HOW TO GUARANTEE YOUR CHILDREN WILL GO TO *Heaven*

Eight Principles for
Parents, Grandparents,
and **Guardians** to
Make Sure Their Kids Are
Successful in Education
and Salvation and
Overcome Temptation

JAMAR HAYNES LEE

WESTBOW
P R E S S®
A DIVISION OF THOMAS NELSON
& ZONDERVAN

Scripture quotes marked (NKJV) are taken from the New King James Version®. Copyright © 1982 by Thomas Nelson. Used by permission. All rights reserved.

Scripture quotations marked (NIV) are taken from the Holy Bible, New International Version®, NIV®. Copyright © 1973, 1978, 1984, 2011 by Biblica, Inc.™ Used by permission of Zondervan. All rights reserved worldwide.

Scripture quotations taken from the Amplified® Bible (AMP), Copyright © 2015 by The Lockman Foundation Used by permission. www.Lockman.org

Scripture quotations taken from the New American Standard Bible® (NASB), Copyright © 1960, 1962, 1963, 1968, 1971, 1972, 1973, 1975, 1977, 1995 by The Lockman Foundation.Used by permission. www.Lockman.org

Scripture quotes marked (KJV) are taken from the King James Version of the Bible.

WestBow Press books may be ordered through booksellers or by contacting:

WestBow Press
A Division of Thomas Nelson & Zondervan
1663 Liberty Drive
Bloomington, IN 47403
www.westbowpress.com
1 (866) 928-1240

ISBN: 978-1-5127-8908-9 (sc)
ISBN: 978-1-5127-8909-6 (hc)
ISBN: 978-1-5127-8907-2 (e)

Library of Congress Control Number: 2017908259

Print information available on the last page.

WestBow Press rev. date: 6/26/2017

This book is dedicated to my lovely wife for life, Cassandra, and our three children, Judah, Jael, and Jedidiah. Without you, this would not have been possible. May the God of our Lord Jesus Christ bless you and keep you throughout eternity.

Contents

Introduction

"In the US 88% of children raised in Evangelical homes leave church at the age of 18, never to return" (Comfort, 2013). Do you want to guarantee your child or grandchild does not fall prey to this statistic? When we apply the principles in this book, we will turn this nation around so that 88 percent of our children never leave Christ, and by age eighteen, they are top performers in education and are bringing others into a relationship with God through His Son, Jesus Christ.

In this book, the scriptures are written out instead of just referenced. This is so that you can use this book as a daily devotion for yourself and your children age ten and older. In this book, I often use the word *parent* when referring to the guardian of a child. However, in the context of this book, "parent" can refer to a grandparent, aunt, uncle, guardian, or anyone who takes care of a child. Doctors have proven that boys and girls are different in many ways, yet this book can be equally applied to both genders whether I use the masculine or feminine pronouns. This book is designed to be used as a daily devotional as well as a self-improvement book. Often, individuals receive God's Word daily but do not feel they have time for another book. However, many people read books to improve their lives but feel they don't have time to read God's Word found in the Bible. As a result of reading this book, you'll be receiving both. Your life will not only be transformed by the information but revolutionized by the revelation God brings as you read His Holy Scriptures documented in this book.

Most would agree that we can learn from our mistakes as well as the mistakes of others. Although we greatly benefit from those who have done things the wrong way, what we really need to learn is how to do things the right way. I could give you a set of house keys and tell you to try each one on each door in the house until you find the right one, but wouldn't it be more beneficial to hand you the right key so you can get it right the first time? This book is a combination of information from those who have championed thriving families and counseled hundreds of thousands successfully. It also contains revelation from God that can change our generations for the better.

"For parents who believe passionately in Jesus Christ and anticipate His promised gift of eternal life, there is no higher priority in life than providing effective spiritual training at home. Unless we are successful in introducing our children to Him, we will never see them again in the afterlife. Everything else is of lesser priority" (Dobson, 2014).

Part I

Why Are Parents Failing?

Chapter 1

The Number-One Responsibility of a Parent

"Do not provoke your children to wrath, but bring them
up in the training and admonition of the Lord"
Ephesians 6:4 (NKJV).

What is the number-one responsibility of a parent? I want you to answer this question by speaking your answer out loud first. Then you can look in this book to see if you answered correctly. Will you change your answer after you read this?

I asked several Christians this question. Here are some of the responses I received.

- help our children get a good education
- protect our children and keep them safe
- provide food and shelter for our children
- teach our children to be good people

All these things mentioned are important, but they are not correct, because they are all temporary. The number-one responsibility of a parent is to prepare his or her children for eternity. This means training them to have a relationship with God through His Son, the Lord Jesus Christ.

In May 2013, a tornado hit the state of Oklahoma and twenty-four people were killed. Among them was twenty-nine-year-old Megan Futrell, who was found holding her five-month-old baby, Case Futrell. I was moved when I heard her story and comforted to know that she was an active church member. She left behind one other child and her husband. This event speaks loudly and clearly to all of us and should put everything in perspective. We can do our best to provide our children with shelter, food, health, a good education, scholarship, and even moral values. But in one moment, all that can be taken away—and the only thing that matters is if our sons or daughters are right with God. Then we can look forward to seeing them again.

Consider this passage: "Fathers, do not provoke your children to wrath, but bring them up in the training and admonition of the Lord" (Ephesians 6:4 NKJV). This scripture applies to mothers as well, especially when the father is not there.

First, we need to understand that we can ensure our children will get saved and live saved lives. I know this goes against mainstream theology, but that is what makes this message revolutionary. Test it by the Spirit and by the Word of God, as well as by your mind. God would not tell us to "bring them up in the training and admonition of the Lord" if we were not able. He confirms that it is possible with other passages.

> These are the commands, decrees, and laws the LORD your God directed me to teach you … so that you, your children and their children after them may fear the LORD your God as long as you live by keeping all his decrees and commands that I give you, and so that you may enjoy long life. (Deuteronomy 6:1–2 NIV)

"Pay close attention to yourself and to your teaching; persevere in these things, for as you do this you will ensure salvation both for yourself and for those who hear you" (1 Timothy 4:16 NASB).

"So they said, 'Believe on the Lord Jesus Christ, and you will be saved, you and your household'" (Acts 16:31 NKJV).

"And she made a vow, saying, 'O Lord Almighty, if you will only look upon your servant's misery and remember me, and not forget your servant but give her a son, then I will give him to the Lord for all the days of his life'" (1 Samuel 1:11 NIV).

If Hannah, Samuel's mother, can make sure her child served the Lord all the days of his life in the Old Testament, how much more can we do it in the New Testament?

Paul said to Timothy, "From infancy you have known the Holy Scriptures, which are able to make you wise for salvation through faith in Christ Jesus" (1 Timothy 3:15 NIV).

"Do not be deceived, God is not mocked; for whatever a man sows, that he will also reap. For he who sows to his flesh will of the flesh reap corruption, but he who sows to the Spirit will of the Spirit reap everlasting life" (Galatians 6:7–8 NKJV). We will go further into this scripture later.

"Train up a child in the way he should go, And when he is old he will not depart from it" (Proverbs 22:6 NKJV).

Proverbs 22:6 has had a lot of controversy over whether it is a promise or a probability. God called me to preach that it is a promise, and everyone who follows the steps in this book will receive that promise. You may ask, "Why have so many kids who have been trained in church departed?" Good question. Think about it. Were the children really trained in the way they should go?

All my life growing up in the church, I heard this popular scripture. Can you finish this verse? "Give us this day our ..." (Matthew 6:11 KJV). Did you get the answer? If you said "daily bread," you are correct! That verse is often said in church services around the world.

The Lord told me that one major problem in the church is that we are not giving our children daily bread. Even though this is one of the most well-known passages quoted in the Bible, the majority of the body of Christ is not doing it. My eleven-year-old son was with me when I shared that revelation with a woman in my neighborhood outside our house. The woman broke down into tears and said that was a word from God. She said she would tell her daughter right away because she wanted her daughter to start reading God's Word daily with her granddaughter.

God is requiring us to speak His Word to our children every day and give them daily bread. This means that if you are not training your children to read God's Word daily, then you are actually training them not to read God's Word daily!

We are training our children no matter what. The question is what are we training them to do? Or what are we training them not to do? Since most Christians are training their children not to read the Bible every day, it is hard even to get adults who are saved and grew up in the church to read God's Word daily; this is because they have to break the habit of not doing it.

Reading God's Word alone is not enough to guarantee that your children will go to heaven—or this book would be over already. But I can't stress enough how important it is. It is as important as providing them food and water daily. "Jesus declared, 'I am the bread of life. Whoever comes to me will never go hungry, and whoever believes in me will never be thirsty'" (John 6:35 NIV).

Dr. James Dobson, the founder of Focus on the Family, quoted Proverbs 22:6 and Ephesians 6:4 and said, "Do they mean that a child should be taught to revere God and His Son, Jesus Christ, and to understand the spiritual dimension of life? Yes, that is their first and most important meaning" (Dobson, *Bringing Up Girls*, 2014).

I would like to address a way of thinking that many Christian parents have been tricked into. Many parents have been tricked into thinking that we should not force our children to participate in spiritual things. We should not force our children to read the Bible, pray, or help the less fortunate. This is the furthest thing from the truth. Any good parent forces his or her children to do what is good.

Do you force your children to eat vegetables and drink water? Do you force them to brush their teeth? Do you force your children to do their homework? Do you force your children to go to bed and to wake up at a certain time? Do you force your children to stop bad behavior? Every good parent would answer yes to these questions. Whatever we force our children to do is what we are training them to do. Therefore, we should train them to read the Word daily, spend time with God daily, and give to others.

Yet, even though we train or force our children to do these things, we should try to make it as pleasant as possible. For example, try to get a vegetable they like, try to have them drink water early so they crave it, and read fun books to them so they develop a joy for reading. We must train our children to do these things. Whatever we train them to do on a daily basis, they will do on a daily basis.

The problem is that we require our children to study for a new test, but we don't require them to study the New Testament. We require our children to spend time doing homework, but we don't require them to spend time with God at home. We give them gifts, but we don't train them how to properly give to others. Therefore, are we really training our children in the way they should go? We are not. Our actions speak louder than our words. It is as if we are sitting our children down and saying, "School and other things are more important; that is why we require you to do your homework and practice extracurricular activities daily. But spiritual things are not as important; therefore, we don't require you to do them daily." We must repent and change the way we are training our children.

My wife has read to our children daily in the morning and I have read to them at night since they were infants. When they became eight years old, she stopped reading with them in the morning. Why? Because they read the Bible and prayed on their own. Now we just ask them what they read about in the morning to reiterate its importance. We still read and pray as a family at night.

In the book *Keeping Your Kids Christian*, V. Gilbert Beers shares the goals that he and his wife have for their children and grandchildren:

1. As early as possible, I want my children to come to know God through Christ, to accept Jesus as their own personal Savior.
2. I want them to learn to practice the presence of the living God each day. I want them to grow daily to be more Christlike, more godly.
3. I want them to grow to love God's Word and develop habits of daily Bible reading, not merely because they should read it, but because they desire to read it.
4. I want them to cultivate an effective prayer life, and a life of sharing their faith with others, again not because they should do these things but because they truly desire to do them. (Beers, 1990).

Are these your goals for your children? If I were to ask your children, "What is most important to your parents concerning your future?" how would they answer? If they are old enough to understand, ask them when you are at home (not at church), "What do you think is most important to me that you accomplish in life?"

Why does God say your children's salvation is your number-one responsibility as a parent? I'll answer that question with a question. "For what profit is it to a man if he gains the whole world, and loses his own soul?" (Matthew 16:26a NKJV).

What does Jesus say that our Heavenly Father wants from us more than anything? An expert in the law tested Jesus with this question: "Teacher, which is the greatest commandment in the Law?"

Jesus replied, "'Love the Lord your God with all your heart and with all your soul and with all your mind.' This is the first and greatest commandment" (Matthew 22:36–38 NIV).

Since God has made this the greatest commandment, it is the greatest thing we should require of our children, and it is our first responsibility. You can't really force someone to love, but you can show them love and show them how to love.

If you are not sure how to train your child to love God, just keep reading or listening and we'll go over that. Notice I said "train your child" instead of "teach your child" how to love God. Many parents think they are training their children when all they are really doing is teaching. But we'll discuss that in a later chapter.

Never forget, the number-one responsibility of a parent is to prepare his or her children for eternity. This means training them to have a relationship with God through His Son, the Lord Jesus Christ. Nothing else compares. Many other things are important but not nearly as important as our children entering God's kingdom. "Seek first the kingdom of God and His righteousness, and all these things shall be added to you" (Matthew 6:33 NKJV).

Chapter 2

Give Us This Day Our Daily Bread

Give us this day our daily bread.
—Matthew 6:11 (NKJV)

Have you ever wondered why currently most children raised in church do not remain committed to God throughout their lives? Some never commit their lives to God. Others get saved and then leave a close relationship with God and live in sin. Sometimes they come back to God after making a lot of bad decisions and experiencing the consequences. I did not want that for my children, and I don't believe any Christian parent does. So I asked God if it was possible to make sure my children gave their lives to Christ at an early age, remained committed to God, and never lived a life of sin. God answered me.

Yes, it is possible! God revealed to me that it was not only possible but that it was a requirement. God showed me that if we follow His commands He *guarantees* our children will maintain a love relationship with Him from birth until burial. Even though our children will sin— "For all have sinned and fall short of the glory of God" (Romans 3:23 NKJV)—they will not live a life of sin or commit the worst sins that lead to death, such as murder, abortion, suicide, promiscuity, homosexual acts, adultery, and so on. You can also find more sins that lead to death in Leviticus 20. "If you see any brother or sister commit a sin that does not lead to death, you should pray and God will give them life. I refer to those whose sin does not lead to death. There is a sin that leads to death. I am not saying that you should pray about that. All wrongdoing is sin, and there is sin that does not lead to death" (1 John 5:16–17 NIV).

God has commissioned me to write this book so all of the body of Christ would know that we can guarantee our children choose Christ for life. I am called to bring this good news that if we follow these directives in this book, we can have children who will never get drunk, do illicit drugs, have sex before marriage (but pursue purity), or commit homosexual acts, idolatry, murder, or suicide. Most important, we will have children who fulfill the greatest commandments by loving God with all their heart, soul, and strength and loving their neighbor as themselves (Matthew 22:36–40). Many have already produced children just like this, and now it is time for *all* the parents in the body of Christ to produce these children.

We can start producing these children by making sure they receive daily bread. Daily bread is reading the Holy Scriptures found in the Bible daily. "Man shall not live by bread alone, but by every word that proceeds from the mouth of God" (Matthew 4:4 and Deuteronomy 8:3 NKJV). Since this is the case, I will take this time to ask you, "Are you reading God's Word to the children you are in charge of daily? Did you do it yesterday? Will you start today? Will you make a time to do it daily?" Someone told me they would try to find time, but that doesn't work. You must *make* time for things that are important, because if you try to find time, you may be looking for a long time.

Matthew 4:4, which we just read, tells us that the words God has spoken are spiritual food necessary for our spirit to live, just as natural food and water are necessary for our bodies to live. If a parent does not feed his or her child for two days with natural food, is that abuse? Similarly, do you go two days out of the week without spiritually feeding your child God's Word? Then aren't you spiritually abusing them? Think about it.

If children do not receive good food regularly, they will die. According to the World Food Program, 3.1 million children in the world under age five die each year from poor nutrition (WFP, 2015). That is over five children every minute. Jesus said in the same way, our children will die spiritually if they do not received God's Word regularly. "Man shall not live by bread alone, but by every word that proceeds from the mouth of God" (Matthew 4:4, Deuteronomy 8:3 NKJV). In other words, Jesus let us know in advance that if we are only giving our children God's Word once or twice a week at church, then they will not live spiritually. That is not enough nourishment.

We must obey the teaching of the Bible, which is that the Word of God is as important as natural food. We need to feed our children's spirits like food to the body, and we must feed our children on a daily basis. In this area, we have been hearers of the Word but not doers, deceiving ourselves (James 1:22). You may be wondering, *Is it really that important that we feed our children the Word of God daily? If we don't read the Bible to them daily or require them to read it, are we really starving our child spiritually? Should we prioritize God's word as we do food?*

What does the Bible say? Job 23:12 (NIV) says, "I have not departed from the commands of his lips; I have treasured the words of his mouth more than my daily bread." Then Jeremiah 15:16 says, "When your words came, I ate them; they were my joy and my heart's delight, for I bear your name, O Lord God Almighty." Psalm 119:103 says, "How sweet are your words to my taste, sweeter than honey to my mouth!"

You may still be asking, "Am I really starving my children because I don't take the time to read the Word of God to them at home every day, yet I prepare a natural meal for them every day?" You may not be convinced it is equal to natural food, but it absolutely is. Jesus is the Word that became flesh (John 1:14). In John 6:35 (NIV), "Jesus declared, 'I am the bread of life. Whoever comes to me will never go hungry, and whoever believes in me will never be thirsty.'"

These scriptures also confirm God's Word is equivalent to natural food. In 1 Peter 2:2–3 (NIV), it says, "Like newborn babies, crave pure spiritual milk, so that by it you may grow up in your salvation, now that you have tasted that the Lord is good." And Hebrews 5:12 (NIV) says, "In fact, though by this time you ought to be teachers, you need someone to teach you the elementary truths of God's word all over again. You need milk, not solid food!"

If you did not know that God required you to give your children daily bread or you just were not doing it, now is the time to repent. Repent to God and to your children and begin today. Your children and your children's children will be changed for generations to come. By giving them their daily bread, you will automatically be getting your daily bread. If you want your children to live spiritually, you must apply the Word. Bishop T. D. Jakes said, "The Word will work if you work it."

Romans 1:17b (NKJV) says, "The just shall live by faith." How do we give our children faith? Romans 10:17 (NKJV) says, "So then faith comes by hearing, and hearing by the word of God." If they are not hearing the word of God daily, how can we expect them to live by faith daily?

If you have not been feeding your child spiritually, there is a simple solution. Repent! Ask your child to forgive you and God to forgive you and start reading the Word of God with your child today (appropriate to his or her age group). "If we confess our sins, he is faithful and just to forgive us our sins, and to cleanse us from all unrighteousness" (1 John 1:9 NKJV). Note—be careful which children's Bible you choose because some of them have pictures that portray people of color in a negative way, for example, Goliath, bandits, and servants are all brown skinned. This can continue to cause races to have an unhealthy fear and negative view of people of color. This is a systemic problem that we all need to help change. We can start by not feeding our children racist and biased images that can even be found in our Bibles.

The Bible says the Word of God will wash you. "Husbands, love your wives, just as Christ also loved the church and gave Himself for her, that He might sanctify and cleanse her with the washing of water by the word" (Ephesians 5:25–26 NKJV). We can wash our spouses or our children with the Word. And we should wash them daily just like washing our bodies or brushing our teeth.

One time as a child, I was out with my aunt Valorie and cousins. I had a red slushy and my teeth got all red, but I thought that was so cool. I said, "Look, everybody, my teeth are red!"

Then my aunt said with a disappointed face, "Jamar, that means you did not brush your teeth!"

I closed my mouth immediately and was afraid to even laugh after that. I had a whole new desire to make sure I brushed my teeth in the morning.

When you brush your teeth, it causes other things not to stick to them. In the same way, when you wash your children in the Word in the morning, you cause things of the world not to stick to them. They may see others smoking or drinking, but it won't stick. They may hear a bad song, but it won't stick. They may see a lustful image, but *it won't stick! Glory to God, it won't stick!*

You may say, "I know of people who read the Bible to their children daily and their children still lived in sin." This can happen. Remember reading the Word daily is just one thing that is critical to guarantee your children are going to heaven. It is definitely not the only thing. If that were the case, this book would be a lot shorter. However, reading God's Word daily is like gasoline in the car; without it, there is no guarantee it will work. Similar to a car, there are many components that we need to have to make this work. You might be thinking, *I know people who only read the Bible to their kids at church on Sunday or not at all, and their children still remained fully committed to the Lord on their own.* We will discuss how this can happen as well.

All children are different. Some children will decide to live a life for Christ no matter what their parents do. Their parents could be an alcoholic, abuser, drug addict, or even of a different faith and threaten to kill their child for believing in Christ (which does happen), and the child could still remain committed to Jesus. Children will make their choice. This book is about God's guarantee and what a Christian parent can do to have it. If the Christian does not obey what God says about daily bread, then they nullify the guarantee that their child will live for Christ. On the other hand, if you do not do these things, it does not mean your children are not going to go to heaven. They will still have to make their own choice.

Consider this analogy. When you go bowling, you can put up the fences to guarantee your ball does not enter the gutter. Of course, if you don't, you still may not get a gutter ball; you could still get a strike. With the fences, your bowling ball is going to get at least one pin. As a parent, when you obey God concerning your child's training as laid out in this book, it is like you are putting up fences to prevent your child from going into the gutter. The gutter would represent eternal separation from God. The pins would represent the many rewards you can receive in heaven. With the fences up, your child may still decide how many pins he or she gets, but at least you know he or she will get into heaven.

Not giving our children daily bread is one major reason that the majority of our youth have been dead spiritually at one time or another. Please give your children the Word daily. In his book *Distortion: The Vanity of Genetically Altered Christianity*, Jesse Duplantis said, "The Word isn't just 'words.' It is actually part of who God is. John 1:1 (NKJV) puts it this way 'In the beginning was the Word, and the Word was with God, and the Word was God'" (Duplantis, 2012). When you give children the Word daily, you give them God daily, and trust me; they need God daily.

Chapter 3

The Commandment
Greater Than "the Ten"

> So that you, your children and their children after them
> may fear the Lord your God as long as you live by keeping
> all his decrees and commands that I give you, and so that
> you may enjoy long life. —Deuteronomy 6:2 (NIV)

Wow! Did you see what God just said? He said there is a way that you, your children, and their children after them will reverence the true God as long as you live; it is by keeping His commandments. Do you want to know how to make that happen? Let's rally around this scripture and find out how God tells us to get these results. That is what this chapter is all about.

Did you know that the commandments are not all equal? Did you know that the Ten Commandments do not even include the greatest and most important commandment? You may be wondering what the greatest commandment is. As mentioned earlier, let's again ask our Lord and Savior Jesus Himself. In Matthew 22:35–38 (NIV) it says,

> An expert in the law, tested him (Jesus) with this question: "Teacher, which is the greatest commandment in the Law?"
>
> Jesus replied: "'Love the Lord your God with all your heart and with all your soul and with all your

mind.' This is the first and greatest commandment. And the second is like it: 'Love your neighbor as yourself.' All the Law and the Prophets hang on these two commandments."

Even though the Bible can and has been used to promote evil acts, the true principles of the Holy Scripture, when used correctly, will always revolve around these two principles:

1. Love God.
2. Love your neighbor as yourself.

Jesus also put the second principle like this: "Treat others the way you want them to treat you" (Luke 6:31 NASB).

When Jesus quoted the greatest commandment, He was quoting Deuteronomy 6:5. This commandment in chapter 6 is critical. It is important to note that when Jesus was tempted by the devil, He quoted three verses to defeat Satan: Deuteronomy 8:3, 6:13, and 6:16. Two of these verses were from Deuteronomy 6, which tells us that if we want to do what Jesus did, we should pay close attention to this chapter in the Bible.

Many times, Jesus answered a question with a question. Sometimes Jesus would give a parable for the people to interpret, but not this time. He answered the question quickly, clearly, and plainly without any cause for confusion. In the original Hebrew text, there were no numbers separating the verses. In Matthew 22, when Jesus quoted the greatest commandment in the whole Bible, He only quoted the first portion of it, which He did often (Matthew 4:4, Luke 4:8). Since our Lord Jesus himself said this is the greatest commandment, then it is important for us to know the entire commandment and obey it. Here is that entire commandment found in Deuteronomy 6 (NIV):

Love the Lord your God with all your heart and with all your soul and with all your strength. These commandments that I give you today are to be upon your hearts. Impress them on your children. Talk about them when you sit at home and when you walk along the road, when you lie down and when you get up. Tie them as symbols on your hands and bind them on your foreheads. Write them on the doorframes of your houses and on your gates.

That is the whole commandment that Jesus said was the greatest commandment in the Bible. Many people have not even heard that entire commandment. Some who have heard it did not know Jesus said it was more important than the Ten Commandments, which are found in Exodus 20:1–17 and Deuteronomy 5:4–21. The Bible tells you what will happen if you obey this greatest commandment; it is a commandment with promise. As we read earlier, verse 2 has a promise: "So that you, your children and their children after them may fear the Lord your God as long as you live by keeping all his decrees and commands that I give you, and so that you may enjoy long life." God goes so far as to say if you obey this you will not even have to worry about your grandchildren fearing the Lord and keeping His commandments.

Since it is the greatest and most important commandment, let's break it down into practical applications. Verse 6 says,

These commandments that I give you today are to be upon your hearts

The *heart* refers to your mind. Another way to read this scripture is, "These commandments are to be on your mind." The reason we are not going over scriptures with our children (or grandchildren and so on) is because it is not on our minds. Most Christian parents are very concerned about their children. We have a lot on our minds concerning our children. What will they eat for breakfast, lunch, and dinner? Did they finish their homework? What time is practice, and do they have all their necessary gear? How are they doing in school? What will they wear for church? How is their health? And the list goes on.

As a result of these things on our minds, every day we ask our children, "Did you finish your food? How was school? Did you finish your homework? How was practice?" These are great questions that should be asked every day. However, we also need to ask them, "Did you read your Bible today? Did you spend time in prayer today? Can I hear your memory verses?" If you are obeying this command and these things are on your heart, then you will ask these kinds of questions daily also. Remember, this is a command and part of the greatest commandment in the Bible. We are commanded to have these things on our hearts.

This is knowledge that every person should have. Please help others and pass this information along, Ask people, "Do you know what the greatest commandment is?" If they don't know, then tell them the answer and the reference found in Deuteronomy 6:4–9. Asking others if they know this scripture is a great way to keep it on your heart and help others do the same.

Impress them on your children

Impress means to implant firmly in the mind or fix in the memory (yourdictionary.com). This is saying that our children should be required to read the principles of the Bible and memorize scripture, just as we require them to clean up, eat their vegetables, or go to school. This is a command.

Talk about them

"Them" refers to all the commandments, principles, and scriptures of the Bible (that's why it says "These are the commands, decrees and laws the Lord your God directed me to teach" (Deuteronomy 6:1)). Many parents don't talk about the commandments except on the day they have church. That will not guarantee you produce a child who remains committed to the Lord from birth until burial. Here are some practical examples of talking about the commandments: Have your child learn a scripture by repeating after you ten times or more. Repetition is the best teacher. Often tell your child to quote the scriptures they have memorized, because if they don't repeat them often, then they will forget them and so will we. If you don't have any memorized, then you can have the pleasure of learning together. Read the Bible to them, and ask them questions afterward to see what they learned. Sing a Christian song together, and talk about its meaning. These are only a few options, but we must incorporate these things on a *daily basis* if we want the promise that our children and grandchildren will fear the Lord and keep His commandments all of our lives.

With our fast-paced society, the question is, when will I be able to do all of these things? The Bible is very specific and detailed as to when and where we should do these things. Let's continue on this journey and discover when the Bible says we should apply the directions given in the previous paragraphs.

When you sit at home

Do you talk about the things of God to your children? Many parents don't even sit and talk to their children. But the Bible commands us to sit and spend some time talking to our children about His commands at home. You can do this in many different ways. Set a time to do it each night. Sometimes you can also incorporate God's principles when you are watching a TV show or a movie together and someone does something wrong or right on TV. You can sometimes press pause and begin talking to your children about it. Ask your children what the person on TV did wrong or right? What should he or she have done? What do they think will happen? How did this make God feel? You can also ask your child, "Why do you think God wants us to do it this way?" You should point out when people do good things on TV and let your children know you are happy when they do these things. Explain to your children why we should do them and the rewards of doing them. It is important to explain to your children why you require them to do something and why you don't allow them to do something. Don't just say, "Because I said so," all the time. It is easier for them to obey your commands when they understand why. Ask them to quote their scriptures while you're at home. This will help them remember those scriptures forever and keep them on their minds.

When you ask your children about their day, you should ask them questions and wait for the answers. Apply James 1:19 (NIV): "Be quick to listen, slow to speak, and slow to become angry." Say to them, "Tell me about your day," and force them to respond. Don't accept answers like, "We didn't do anything." If you have enough patience, eventually they will let you in their world. Many times when our children are ready to speak, it seems inconvenient for us, but sometimes we need to stop what we are doing and listen when our children have something on their heart. "Therefore, as we have opportunity, let us do good to all people, especially to those who belong to the family of believers" (Galatians 6:10 NIV), starting with your own family.

When you walk along the road

Walking was the main form of transportation in biblical times. Now, of course, we have many other ways of traveling on the road. It is important for us to know that the Bible commands us to talk about God's commandments when we are on the road, in the car, on the bus, in a plane, and so on. In your fifteen-minute car ride, your children could learn a new scripture, repeat the ones they know, go over a Bible lesson, or talk about what they learned from the Bible that day. The Bible doesn't say you must do it every time you are on the road, but it does imply that it should be done regularly when you are on the road.

When you lie down

Read a Bible story from a children's Bible before they go to bed. Say a prayer together, and let them lead the prayer sometimes. This is so important to do while they are young so they won't have a problem doing it when they are older. But whatever the age, if they are in your home, you should require them to take time out for God's Word. Before our kids went to bed, I shut everything down, TV and electronics, for myself and the kids. The kids, my wife, and I would read the Bible and pray together. Sometimes it was thirty minutes, and sometimes it was only a few minutes. Let the Holy Spirit lead you and give the Spirit time to have His way. "But as for me and my household, we will serve the Lord" (Joshua 24:15 NIV). Don't just send your kids to bed; put them to bed with a consistent routine, including the Bible and prayer together. Pray a blessing over them before they go to bed.

When you get up

One principle that should definitely be applied is "Seek first the kingdom of God and His righteousness, and all these things shall be added to you" (Matthew 6:33 NKJV). Remember, this needs to be impressed on our children. Therefore, we need to pray with them when we get up or train them to do it when they get up. Read God's word in the morning and train your children to do the same. Sometimes you can have them lead the morning prayer. When I went to work, my wife was the one who prayed and read the Bible with our children in the morning. She did this until they became old enough to do it on their own, and they desired to do it. My son asked me if he could create his own prayer when he was nine, and I was elated to let him.

The same way you make sure your kids eat breakfast and drink juice or water in the morning, you should make sure they pray and read God's Word in the morning. If you are reading this and you do not pray with your kids and read God's Word (or make sure they do it) when they get up, start today. This principle alone of seeking first the kingdom of God and His righteousness will change your life as you watch God add to you everything you need. That's His promise, not mine.

Tie them as symbols on your hands

In Jewish tradition, many took this scripture literally. They would write Deuteronomy 6:4–9 and other scriptures on separate strips of parchment and place them in two small leather boxes called *phylacteries*. The observant Jew would strap it on his forehead and left arm. Fortunately, the commandment is not requiring us to do that. We use our hands to do almost everything, and this scripture is saying we should involve God's commandments in everything we do. We should constantly be reminded of God's ways. In addition, we should use our hands to do spiritual things like blessing our children, praying, and helping those in need. We use our hands to buy everything we buy, and we should use our hands to buy a children's Bible for our children. Your hands may even be used to turn the pages or scroll this book or push play on your audio system. No matter what you do with your hands, it should line up with God's principles. Similar to a wedding ring, which reminds us of our covenant in marriage, we should constantly remember our covenant with God as we use our hands daily.

Bind them on your foreheads

Your forehead contains the part of your brain called the prefrontal cortex. "The prefrontal cortex is where you make decisions to take action on a thought. The prefrontal cortex handles your behavior!" (therefinersfire. org, 2016). Therefore "bind them on your foreheads" is saying to use the scriptures to make every decision. What music can your children listen to? What TV shows and movies can they watch? Whom are they allowed to spend time with? What school will they attend? If it influences them away from God's commands, just say *no*. If it lines up with God's will, say yes. Use the scriptures to make every decision.

Write them on the doorframes of your houses

Many Jews literally take small containers called *mezuzot*, place scripture passages in them, and attach them to their doorframes (NASB, 1999). It is critical to understand the priority that God has given to the scriptures. Not only are the scriptures supposed to be on your agenda, but they are supposed to be first on your agenda. As parents, we have a lot of obligations for each child. God knows we have to fulfill our other obligations, but the first one we need to fulfill is the spiritual obligation of going over God's Word and demonstrating it. We consider ourselves good, godly parents when we require our children to finish their homework and chores before they can watch TV or play. However, God is saying that the scriptures should take priority. Out of all the things we make time for in our house, we must make sure our houses make time for God's Word. Train them to make the Word of God and prayer a top priority in their lives.

Write them ... on your gates

Not literally. To me, this is symbolic of putting a sign on your gate that says to the devil, "No Trespassing"! Take authority over your atmosphere. If it is your property, then it is God's property and everything in it should be subject to the scriptures. My grandad had siblings who were not saved. When they came to visit, they had to leave their alcohol bottles at his gate. He had a standard that people had to adhere to once they came through his gate. We should have a standard inside our gate as well. Of course, we should be hospitable and invite those who are lost to come into our homes, especially our family members (maybe not all our family members). Being hospitable does not mean you have to allow them to curse, smoke, drink, and so on on your property—inside your gates. At the same time, I do believe posting the scriptures on your gates or door can be a blessing.

> "But as for me and my household, we will
> serve the Lord" (Joshua 24:15 NIV).

Ask yourself, "When is the last time I read the Bible to my children and asked them questions? Do I have a set time for a family devotion each day?" Examine yourself and make sure you line up with the most important commandment in the Bible. If you have a child and you are not doing these things currently, begin applying them immediately. Now that you have this knowledge, it changes everything. If you choose not to make time for God's Word when you know He requires it of you and your family daily, then you are choosing to live in sin. "Anyone, then, who knows the good he ought to do and doesn't do it, sins" (James 4:17 NIV). How then could you receive the reward of the righteous?

Let's do what is right and fully obey the greatest commandment. Then we can enjoy long life, having children and grandchildren who fear the Lord as long as we live. Now that is how you get true joy, living the good life. "I have no greater joy than to hear that my children are walking in the truth" (3 John 1:4 NIV).

Chapter 4

Statistics: How Bad Is It?

"When the enemy comes in like a flood, the Spirit of
the LORD will lift up a standard against him"
Isaiah 59:19 (NKJV)

T he predicament of our Christian youth is worse in some areas
than others around the globe. Although these principles can
be applied all over the world, let us look at these statistics in
the United States:

In the book *Battle Cry for a Generation* (2005), Ron Luce presents a
table from the book *The Bridger Generation* by Thom S. Rainer. The
following are from that table:

- The Builders were born between 1927 and 1945. Out of those
  born during that time, 65 percent were Bible-based believers in
  the United States of America.
- Boomers were born from 1946 to 1964. They had 35 percent
  Bible-based believers. The amount was cut by about half.
- Busters were born from 1965 to 1983. They had 16 percent
  Bible-based believers.
- Bridgers were born from 1984 and after. Only 4 percent of them
  affirm to be church-attending Bible-based believers. (Luce, 2005).

The clock is ticking! We must start now, while we still have a chance to turn this around.

For the Millennials born after 2000, the pattern has not stopped. Even a study published November 2015 stated the "recent decrease in religious beliefs and behaviors is largely attributable to the 'nones'—the growing minority of Americans, particularly in the Millennial generation, who say they do not belong to any organized faith … Altogether, the religiously unaffiliated (also called the "nones") now account for 23% of the adult population, up from 16% in 2007." This study was published by the Pew Research Center (Pew Center, 2015).

"I have this [charge] against you, that you have left your first love [you have lost the depth of love that you first had for Me]. So remember the heights from which you have fallen, and repent [change your inner self—your old way of thinking, your sinful behavior—seek God's will] and do the works you did at first [when you first knew Me]; otherwise, I will visit you and remove your lampstand (the church, its impact) from its place—unless you repent" (Revelation 2:4–5 AMP).

In the year 2000, some 240,000 children were born to girls age eighteen or younger. Since 2005, every day, eight thousand teenagers in the United States become infected by an STD—eight thousand teenagers a day! (Luce, 2005).

In 2016, the US Department of Health and Human Services posted, "Adolescents ages 15–24 account for nearly half of the 20 million new cases of STDs each year." Today, four in ten sexually active teen girls have had an STD that can cause infertility and even death. The most effective way to prevent STDs is to abstain from sexual activity."

While many youth are destroying their lives through sexual immorality, the enemy has also caused many youth lives to be cut short through suicide. Here are more alarming statistics documented by the Centers for Disease Control Prevention in April 2016.

Since 2011, the second leading cause of death for those between the ages of fifteen and thirty-four was suicide (the first leading cause of death has consistently been unintentional injury). The suicides have been steadily increasing for years.

- 2011—10,922
- 2012—11,088
- 2013—11,226
- 2014—11,648

The third leading cause of death has been homicides, consistently right behind suicides (Centers for Disease Control and Prevention, 2016; Dykman, 2008).

Our society is screaming for help. With 11,648 suicides in 2014 for those between the ages of fifteen and thirty-four, that is *over thirty suicides a day! That is over nine hundred a month*! Selah (pause and think about that)! The church youth should be the ones answering the call and helping other youth find their purpose in God's love. However, instead of the church youth bringing others in, the vast majority are being taken out.

According to a *Time* magazine article, published March 10, 2008, by Jackson Dykman, "The fastest growing religious group is people without any religious affiliation" (Dykman, 2008).

In the 2016 winter issue of Ohio Christian University's magazine, President Dr. Mark A. Smith stated that "over the last five years, more than 100,000 churches closed and in the next five years more than 100,000 more churches will close … 1,700 pastors leave ministry every month" (Smith, 2016).

The enemy has obviously come in, but "When the enemy comes in like a flood, the Spirit of the LORD will lift up a standard against him" (Isaiah 59:19 NKJV). We will be that standard led by the Spirit of the Lord. Together, we will not lose the next generation to the world.

Our children and grandchildren and those children we have influence over will be used by God to advance the kingdom of heaven. Instead of allowing the enemy to come into our homes and take our children, we will bring God into our homes and train our children to defeat the enemy daily. We will not allow the media and electronic devices to destroy our youth, but we will use those resources to develop our youth for God. Then we will send them out into the world to help save and heal through the power of Jesus Christ. In order to make disciples of all nations, we must start by making disciples of all our children.

"Therefore go and make disciples of all nations, baptizing them in the name of the Father and of the Son and of the Holy Spirit, and teaching them to obey everything I have commanded you" (Matthew 28:19–20a NIV).

True revival will not be on the weekend at church but during the weekdays in our homes. The fire may be lit at a church event, but parents need to add the wood at home for our children to stay on fire for God. When is the last time you had family prayer and family devotions? What time is family prayer at your home? What time is family Bible reading? If you don't have a time set, now is the time to set it. At the bottom of this page, write down the time you will have family devotions (prayer and scripture reading). Just as Jesus told Peter in Matthew 16:18 (NKJV), He is telling you. God wants to use you and your family to build His church, "and the gates of hell shall not prevail against it."

I will have daily family devotion at _____.
Signed by _____. Date_____

According to Ray Comfort, the cohost of the award-winning TV program *Way of the Master* and author of *How to Bring Your Children to Christ … and Keep Them There*, "In 2002 a report released by a major US denomination on family life, claimed, quote, '88% of children raised in Evangelical homes leave church at the age of 18, never to return'" (Comfort, 2013).

"Every year in America, 4.5 million teenagers turn 20 years old. Research shows that once a child reaches that milestone, the odds of reaching that individual for Christ are nearly 10 to 1. In fact, the Barna Research Group has gathered data that leads them to conclude that 'what you believe by the time you're 13 is what you will die believing'" (Luce, 2005).

"Chasten your son while there is hope, And do not set your heart on his destruction" (Proverbs 19:18 NKJV).

The time is now! We should start before it is too late. The earlier the better. This is imperative to guarantee our children remain committed to God for life and go to heaven. With the principles in this book, we can turn the statistics around so that at least 88 percent of all children raised in evangelical homes will never leave Christ and the church but will help build the church by loving God and others.

Part II

Eight Principles for
C.H.I.L.D.R.E.N.

Chapter 5

Commit Each Child to God

When the time of their purification according to the Law
of Moses had been completed, Joseph and Mary took him
(Jesus) to Jerusalem to present him to the Lord."
—Luke 2:22 (NIV)

Jesus is our prime example. He was committed to God. All the firstborn males were committed to God. "You are to give over to the LORD the first offspring of every womb. All the firstborn males of your livestock belong to the LORD ... Redeem every firstborn among your sons" (Exodus 13:12–13b NIV).

"As it is written in the Law of the Lord, Every firstborn male that opens the womb shall be called holy to the Lord" (Luke 2:22–23 NASB).

Under the New Testament covenant, we are all holy, not just the firstborn and not just the males. We are all priests, not just the Levites. We are all royalty because we are children of the King of kings. The Bible says, "But you are a chosen generation, a royal priesthood, a holy nation, His own special people, that you may proclaim the praises of Him who called you out of darkness into His marvelous light" (1 Peter 2:9 NKJV).

Those who are in Christ are all holy unto the Lord. We are a holy nation—not only the firstborn but the second and third and the rest of your children for you super-fruitful saints.

We can have the commitment ceremony soon after the baby is born, but the actual commitment should come before then, when your baby is in the womb. Many women change their whole lifestyle when they find out they are pregnant. They may stop smoking and drinking and start eating healthier foods to have the healthiest baby possible. Spiritually, we should be reading God's Word daily to our children even in the womb. "Around week 16 of pregnancy, it's likely for your baby to start detecting some limited noises. Beginning in the second trimester of pregnancy, your baby can detect sounds from outside your body" (whattoexpect.com, 2015). Therefore if your child can hear after four months in womb and "Faith comes by hearing," then you can start building their faith even in the womb. It does make a difference when you start applying these eight principles.

In order to guarantee your children remain committed to the Lord Jesus Christ and do not live in sin, you need to start applying these principles by three years of age. However, even if you start after three years of age, your child still may stay with Christ and might never live in sin. My point is that based on God's Word and experts on child development, if you do not apply these eight principles by age three or earlier, the results described are not guaranteed. This is because you reap what you sow. I will explain this principle further in chapter 20.

If you have not been sowing the seeds to spend time with God and His Word on a daily basis, then you have been sowing seeds to put something else first on a daily basis. Those seeds will most likely bear fruit. If you have been just going to church every Sunday, then you have been training a weekly religion and not a close daily relationship with God for the first years of the child's life. Starting at least by the age of three is critical, but for the best results, training should start in the womb. The earlier the better!

> A newborn's brain is about 25% of its future adult weight. By the time a child is three years old her brain will have produced billions of cells and hundreds of trillions of

connections, or synapses, between nerve cells ... There are "critical periods" during a child's early years when certain opportunities for learning must be grabbed or forever lost ... If a child is regularly overwhelmed by negative feelings and stressful circumstances, her inability to cope in infancy becomes a life-long pattern. (Dobson, *Bringing Up Girls*, 2014).

An article posted April 16, 2016, titled, "When Does Discipline Begin? An Age-by-Age Guide to Setting Limits," said this, "'Setting limits is a critical part of your responsibility as a parent,' says Claire Lerner, LCSW, director of parenting resources at Zero to Three, in Washington, DC. 'Just keep explaining the rules, and by age 2 1/2 to 3, he'll begin to understand them and be better able to act on them.'" (Lerner, 2016).

Someone may be wondering, "Is it too late for my child, who is already a teenager?" *It is never too late to* commit your children and your household to God. It is only 100 percent guaranteed results if you start by the time they are three, but the earlier you start, the more likely they are to be dedicated to Christ earlier. My dad got saved in his fifties. If your son or daughter or grandchild is in your household, you can still follow these steps whether they are four or forty-four (and I know some of you have your forty-something-year-old son or daughter living with you). Whenever you repent and make this change, tell your child something like, "I'm sorry, I realize I have not fully trained you in the way you should go, but we are all growing. I'm growing and I know more now. From now on, things are going to change." Then follow all these steps and let God do the rest.

"Commit to the LORD whatever you do, and he will establish your plans" (Proverbs 16:3 NIV).

In order to guarantee your child goes to heaven, you need to commit your child to God.

Chapter 6

Holiness Lived in Front of Your Children

Pursue peace with all people, and holiness,
without which no one will see the Lord.
—Hebrews 12:14 (NKJV)

Watch your life and doctrine closely. Persevere in them, because
if you do, you will save both yourself and your hearers.
—1 Timothy 4:16 (NIV)

"**D**o as I say, but not as I do" does not work. We must practice what we preach. This is crucial. Bishop Brian Keith Williams said, "You can teach what you know, but you will reproduce what you are." We must live the life that we want them to live in order to guarantee they will follow Christ from birth until burial. It does not mean that we will not make mistakes; it does mean that when we do make a mistake, we confess it and apologize for it.

We will sin, of course, but we should not commit those sins that lead to death, for example, if you are a married man, flirting with a woman other than your wife is a sin, but if you repent of that sin early on, it will not kill you spiritually. Committing adultery, however, will kill you spiritually (and may lead to your spouse desiring to kill you physically).

> If you see any brother or sister commit a sin that does not lead to death, you should pray and God will give them life. I refer to those whose sin does not lead to death. There is a sin that leads to death. I am not saying that you should pray about that. All wrongdoing is sin, and there is sin that does not lead to death. (1 John 5:16–17 NIV)

If your child is in a two-parent household, both parents need to be a saved example. Otherwise, every day, even without intention, one parent will be sowing a seed into the child that says, "It is not that important to make Jesus your Lord." This still should not stop you from doing all the things in God's Word and emphasized in this book. The more good seeds you sow, the better chance you have of reaping a better harvest in your children.

We are an example to our children whether we want to be or not. It is important that we are a good example to our children. What does being a good example look like?

The Bible describes a good example in 1 Timothy 3 (NIV). It refers to an "overseer," also interpreted as a pastor or bishop. Since we as parents are overseers of our children, it is applicable to us as well. It is written to a man or father, but the principles apply to a woman or mother as well. It reads as follows.

> Now the overseer is to be above reproach, faithful to his wife, temperate, self-controlled, respectable, hospitable, able to teach, not given to drunkenness, not violent but gentle, not quarrelsome, not a lover of money. He must manage his own family well and see that his children obey him, and he must do so in a manner worthy of full respect. (If anyone does not know how to manage his own family, how can he take care of God's church?) He must not be a recent convert, or he may become

conceited and fall under the same judgment as the devil. He must also have a good reputation with outsiders, so that he will not fall into disgrace and into the devil's trap.

In essence, we must be what we want our children to be. Of course we want them to be better than we are, but we must be the mature Christian God wants us to be in order to give them a chance to be better than we are. If you don't want them to smoke, don't smoke.

Not committing sin in front of your children is better than them seeing you commit sin. However, even if you commit sin when they cannot see you, you are still sowing the seeds of sin into your family. Therefore, what you do in the dark could very well show up in the light through your children. After David secretly slept with Uriah's wife and ordered his murder, God said this:

> Thus says the LORD: "Behold, I will raise up adversity against you from your own house; and I will take your wives before your eyes and give them to your neighbor, and he shall lie with your wives in the sight of this sun. For you did it secretly, but I will do this thing before all Israel, before the sun." (2 Samuel 2:11–12 NKJV).

We should be able to say what Paul said, "Follow my example, as I follow the example of Christ" (1 Corinthians 11:1 NIV).

We must live holy lives in front of our children.

You may be thinking, *Why are there so many parents that live holy lives who have children that live hellish ones?* Great question. This leads us to the next step.

Chapter 7

Instruct and Train Your Children

Fathers, do not exasperate your children; instead, bring
them up in the training and instruction of the Lord.
—Ephesians 6:4 (NIV)

Train up a child in the way he should go, And
when he is old he will not depart from it.
—Proverbs 22:6 (NKJV)

I did research to find out what the word *train* meant in the original
Hebrew in this verse. I found out it is the verb חָנַךְ (khanakh),
which means "to train up" (Blue Letter Bible, 2016). In other
words, *train* in the original Hebrew meant exactly what it means in
English, "train".

The definition of *train* is "to give the discipline and instruction, drill,
practice, etc., designed to impart proficiency or efficiency" (dictionary.
com, 2016).

To train a child in the way he should go means to be consistent in the
ways of God on a daily basis. You may teach something one time, but to
train it means to do it over and over and over and over again. This is a
daily thing; it is not a hobby to be performed only once or twice a week.

"Run in such a way as to get the prize. Everyone who competes in the
games goes into strict training. They do it to get a crown that will not

last, but we do it to get a crown that will last forever" (1 Corinthians 9:24b–25 NIV).

As a youth pastor, I see the opposite taking place in our churches. I see parents who have their children spend two hours a day, five days a week training for a sport that is temporary, but they don't have their children spend even five minutes a day for prayer and God's Word, which is eternal. We don't have to give up sports for Christ, but at least two to five minutes a day would be a start (like brushing your teeth or a taking a shower, as mentioned before). Imagine how strong our church families would be if our parents were more concerned about their children's spirits than their sports.

I enjoyed playing sports growing up and later coaching various sports. You can teach your strategy in a classroom or locker room, but you will have to leave the room to train. There are many definitions of "teach," but I'm talking about the most common—to instruct by precept, example, or experience. This is what many Christian parents do, but it is much different from training.

What is the big difference between teaching and training? I will give you an example. You can teach your children how to play basketball from a book, but that will not make them a good basketball player. You can teach them how to play by demonstrating right in front of them, but even if you were the best player in the NBA and played like Michael Jordan, LeBron James, and Kobe Bryant in their prime, teaching them by simply showing them an example of what to do would not be enough to produce a good basketball player. In order to produce a good basketball player, you must give them the ball and let them practice. That is the difference between teaching and training. Now you know how someone can live righteously their whole life, as Samuel did (1 Samuel 12), yet still have children who live in sin. "But his sons did not walk in his ways; they turned aside after dishonest gain, took bribes, and perverted justice" (1 Samuel 8:3 NKJV).

In the same way, bringing your children to church and praising God in front of them is great, but it's not training. Making your child sit in church while the preacher is teaching may be wonderful, but it's not training. Telling your child a Bible story is beneficial, but it is not actually training. Even showing your child what to do, by reading the Bible, praying, fasting, and helping the poor in front of them is being a great example and all these things are necessary; however, it is still not training yet.

You are not training your child until your child is doing the work. "Faith without works is dead" (James 2:26b NKJV). Tell your child, "It's your turn. You lead the prayer. You read the Bible to me, and you tell me what you learned." That is training. Training your child also includes your child visiting those shut in, helping the needy, practicing love and unselfishness, giving, sharing their faith, singing, clapping, and praising God in different ways. Training is taking place when your child is the one doing the work.

Teaching our children to help those in need is critical. As parents, we often try so hard to make sure our children have everything they need that we neglect to teach our children to be concerned about the needs of others. As a result, our children may become selfish or self-absorbed.

In order to teach our children to be concerned about the needs of others, we adopted a child from the organization Compassion.com. Our children were able to write to the child and give some of their money to help the child, who was their age. I encourage all parents to do the same. Not only will you be teaching your children to love others and not to be selfish, but you will be helping a child in desperate need of your help. You will be fulfilling God's will for His people and training your children to do the same.

We also have our children go to the nursing home to sing and visit those shut in. Another idea is a carwash our youth did to help raise money for St. Jude Children's Research Hospital. Mission trips are a great way for our children to participate in helping others. There are many ways to train them to give to others less fortunate. This is an important part of guaranteeing our children go to heaven.

> Jesus said, "Then the King will say to those on his right, 'Come, you who are blessed by my Father; take your inheritance, the kingdom prepared for you since the creation of the world. For I was hungry and you gave me something to eat, I was thirsty and you gave me something to drink, I was a stranger and you invited me in, I needed clothes and you clothed me, I was sick and you looked after me, I was in prison and you came to visit me.'
>
> "Then the righteous will answer him, 'Lord, when did we see you hungry and feed you, or thirsty and give you something to drink? When did we see you a stranger and invite you in, or needing clothes and clothe you? When did we see you sick or in prison and go to visit you?'
>
> "The King will reply, 'Truly I tell you, whatever you did for one of the least of these brothers and sisters of mine, you did for me.'" (Matthew 25:34–40 NIV)

I thought my son was trained on how to pray because I taught him two prayers when he was four years old. So when he was five, I told him to pray for someone out loud. He said, "I don't know what to say." I was tempted to get upset with him and say, "What do you mean you don't know what to say?" If you are a parent, you know the feeling. I didn't question him though. I realized that he wasn't trained like I thought he was, and it was going to take some more practice for him to be proficient at praying out loud. As parents, we have to stop blaming our children for not performing like we expect when we may not have spent enough time training them.

When we potty train our children, we are patient and consistent with them. It may be a short process, or it may be a long one. We should not get upset with them for going on themselves before they are trained. Before we get upset with our children for not doing what we want them to do, we should always examine ourselves and ask ourselves, "Have I spent enough time training my child in this area?" A great speaker named Jim Rohn said, "Children don't lack the capacity to learn; parents lack the time."

You can teach your children in Sunday class and Bible class; however, training takes place at home daily. Whatever you require your children to do in their daily life is what you are training them to do for the rest of their life. Many churchgoing parents have only trained their children to pray at home when they bless their food. That is why there are drug dealers who, even though they deal drugs for a living, bless their food. Why? They were trained to do that.

In addition to requiring our children to bless their food, we must require them to spend time in prayer and Bible reading. You do this by doing it with them and then listening to them pray and read God's Word to you as soon as they can. Try to make it as fun and as relevant as you can.

As parents, we are training our children no matter what. We are training them to develop either good habits or bad habits. Therefore, if we are not training our children to read the Bible and pray every day, then we are actually training them not to pray and read the Bible every day. I repeat—if we are not training them to do it, then we are training them not to do it. And this is our fault.

In order to guarantee your children go to heaven, you must instruct them and train them this way, and when they get old, they won't depart from it.

Chapter 8

Love and Esteem Your Spouse Properly

Husbands, love your wives, just as Christ also
loved the church and gave Himself for her.
—Ephesians 5:25 (NKJV)

And let the wife see that she respects and reverences her
husband [that she honors him, prefers him and esteems him].
—Ephesians 5:33b (AMP)

Why did God make man and woman one through marriage?

Malachi 2:15 (NKJV) says, "But did He not make them (husband and wife) one, Having a remnant of the Spirit? And why one? He seeks godly offspring. Therefore, take heed to your spirit, And let none deal treacherously with the wife of his youth."

One reason God created marriage is because He is seeking "godly offspring." However, you must love your spouse properly to guarantee you will have godly offspring (kids).

Genesis 29:20 and 31 (NIV) says, "So Jacob served seven years to get Rachel, but they seemed like only a few days to him because of his love for her. … When the Lord saw that Leah was not loved, he opened her womb, but Rachel was barren."

Jacob loved Rachel, and they had Joseph and Benjamin together, and as a result, these children lived a life fully committed to the Lord from birth until burial.

Before Joseph and Benjamin, Jacob had ten other children by women he did not love, and those children became adulterers, murderers, and liars. And all of them lived in sin. Why?

One main reason was their mother was not loved.

Samuel's dad loved his mom. In 1 Samuel 1:5 (NKJV), it says, "But to Hannah he (Hannah's husband) would give a double portion, for he loved Hannah, although the Lord had closed her womb."

One reason Samuel was fully committed to the Lord all the days of his life from birth to burial (1 Samuel 12) was because Samuel's father loved his mother.

So why were Samuel's kids wicked?

God revealed to me that Samuel did not love his wife properly. As a result, his children were wicked.

"But his sons did not walk in his ways; they turned aside after dishonest gain, took bribes, and perverted justice" (1 Samuel 8:3 NKJV).

Those of you Bible scholars already know that Samuel's wife is not mentioned in the Bible. Is that a big deal?

Think about it … Who is credited with writing 1 Samuel? (This is not a trick question.) Samuel is credited with writing the majority of 1 Samuel; he could not have written all of it since his death is recorded in 1 Samuel 25.

So Samuel (or possibly another author) mentions the love his dad had for his mom, but he does not mention his love for his own wife. That was his problem. In fact, Samuel does not mention her at all. And a godly husband praises his wife, according to Proverbs 31:28. If he had loved her properly, the Bible would have stated that. But this was revealed to me by the Spirit of God.

The point is Samuel did not love his wife properly, and he ended up with wicked kids.

Samuel grew up with Eli. Samuel did not see Eli love his wife properly (or he would have recorded it like he did with his own parents), and Eli ended up with wicked kids. Eli's wife is not mentioned at all either. Samuel followed Eli's pattern of a husband.

For some reason, at this time, God did not often correct His people for being bad husbands or bad fathers. I admit, I'm not sure why God did that then, but I know what is required of us now. Even though He created one man and one woman in the beginning, later He allowed men to have more than one wife. In 1 Samuel 12:8, He does not chastise David for his other wives but only for taking Uriah's wife. But you cannot love a wife properly if you have more than one.

I often tell young men, "You're not a real man because you can love a million women. A real man can love one woman a million ways."

God corrects this back to His original plan in the New Covenant.

Jesus said, "Have you not read that He who made them at the beginning 'made them male and female,' and said, 'For this reason a man shall leave his father and mother and be joined to his wife, and the two shall become one flesh'?" (Matthew 19:4–5 NKJV).

"A Bishop then must be blameless, the husband of one wife" (1 Timothy 3:2a NKJV).

As you can see, loving your spouse properly is a key ingredient in baking the cake of spiritually successful kids. It is obviously easier said than done when around half of the marriages in the United States end in divorce. One of the number-one reasons given for divorce is financial difficulty. Let's investigate this.

In this day and age, it seems like we never have enough money for our children even though our children have much more than previous generations in comparison. When we don't have enough money to do what the mom or dad wants to do, it can put a strain on the relationship. Even though too many financial arguments go all the way to divorce, it is not really because of lack of finances but because of lack of agreement. The reality is those who are divorced are much worse off financially than those who are married. In order to help with financial oneness, I recommend Dave Ramsey's Financial Peace University. You can try to find a class (or start a class) near you online at daveramsey.com.

The truth is we do not need all the stuff that we think we need. Our marriage is more important than money; our children are more important than money. We must learn to use things and love our spouse, instead of use our spouse and love things. "A few vegetables where there is love are better than the finest meat where there is hatred." (Proverbs 15:17 NIRV).

Single moms or dads, you don't have to be married to train your child in the way they should go. Some women think they need a man, but a bad man is worse than no man at all. Timothy was trained through the faith of his mom and Grandma. Even though he only received his spiritual training from them, Timothy was saved from birth to burial. Single mothers, you can do it too (more on this in chapter 18). Although you do need to put your sons around a godly man, you just don't need to be in a close relationship with that man.

As an encouragement to single dads, Esther was trained and raised by Mordecai, her cousin. Thank God for cousins and other family sometimes stepping in to help raise kids. Mordecai accepted the role of a single father. Not only was she a virgin until she was married, but she fasted and prayed as a young wife, and she still listened to Mordecai's counsel as a married woman. Even being raised by a single man, Esther was righteous from birth until burial (her story is found in the book of Esther). At the same time, you should have your daughter around a godly woman as well, even though you don't need to be in a romantic relationship with that woman. Just like Mordecai, single dads, you can do it too!

You may be wondering, *How do I love my spouse properly? I did not have great examples.* Whether you had great examples or not, you can be given the knowledge and training to love your spouse properly. Just speak their love language on a regular basis.

This section is a great introduction to the five love languages or a great reminder if you are familiar with them. This section is dedicated to Dr. Gary Chapman, whom God used to cause my marriage to continue to flourish!

As a spouse, you need to read (or listen to) the book, *The Five Love Languages* by Dr. Gary Chapman (2015). This knowledge can save you and your spouse years of heartache. God said, "My people are destroyed for lack of knowledge, because they rejected knowledge" (Hosea 4:6 NIV). Don't let your marriage suffer or be destroyed because of your lack knowledge. I can't stress enough the importance of reading the book, and I have been given permission by Dr. Chapman and *The Five Love Languages* publisher to provide some information from the book to help you understand why it is so important.

Every person has a primary language of love, a way in which he or she feels emotional love best. This book will show you how to recognize and speak your spouse's primary love language as well as the four other love languages that can help your spouse know you love him or her. As you will see in the book, you will need to speak your spouse's primary love language in order for him or her to feel loved. Here are the five love languages and a brief description.

Words of Affirmation

If this is your love language, words that are very important to you include *please*, *thank you*, and *I love you*. Compliments and words of appreciation go a long way.

You can become intensely hurt or upset by being told to do something instead of asked to do something and by hearing insults or complaints.

Quality Time

If this is your love language, it is very important to you to spend quality time with the person you love. It is also necessary sometimes to have that quality time without distractions from TV, phones, PCs, chores, food, or other things.

You can become intensely hurt or upset when the person you want to love does not make time for you, talk about his or her feelings, or listen to you with undivided attention.

Physical Touch

If this is your love language, you desire to express love through hugs, kisses, holding one another, and other forms of appropriate touching.

You can be intensely hurt or upset by physical abuse, infidelity, neglect, or the lack of physical presence.

Receiving Gifts

If this is your love language, you feel loved and express love through gifts. The thoughtfulness and effort behind a gift is just as important as the gift. You also feel more loved by the gift of presence, which is the physical presence of a loved one during special events.

You can be intensely hurt or upset by a missed birthday, anniversary, baby's birth, holiday, church service, and so on or a thoughtless gift.

Acts of Service

If this is your love language, you feel most loved when someone is doing something for you. Vacuuming, doing the dishes, laundry, cooking, and helping with other chores around the house are true expressions of love.

You can be intensely hurt or upset by laziness, broken commitments, or when the one you love does not do specific chores you requested.

Before *The Five Love Languages*, I told my wife she had overdosed on shoes and I wasn't going to support her addiction. After *The Five Love Languages*, I realized that shoes were one way she really felt loved; therefore I told my wife she couldn't have enough shoes. I began to put an amount in the budget for her to buy stuff for her, me, and the kids. After *The Five Love Languages*, she stopped trying to tell me what to do and started asking me to do what she would like me to do. It revolutionized our marriage and our life. Thank you, God, and thank you, Dr. Chapman!

If you are married, in order to guarantee your children will go to heaven, you need to love your spouse properly.

Chapter 9

Declare Your Children's Future

Therefore, the promise comes by faith, so that it may be by grace and may be guaranteed to all Abraham's offspring—not only to those who are of the law but also to those who have the faith of Abraham. He is the father of us all … (as it is written, "I have made you a father of many nations") in the presence of Him whom he believed—God, who gives life to the dead and calls those things which do not exist as though they did."
—Romans 4:16 (NIV), 4:17 (NKJV)

Jesus said, "Whoever does not doubt in his heart, but believes that those things he says will be done, he will have whatever he says."
—Mark 11:23b (NKJV).

Declaring your child's future is also known as a prophetic blessing. In the profound book, *The Power of the Prophetic Blessing* by John Hagee, it states, "The Prophetic Blessing is a spoken declaration by a spiritual authority over the life of an individual. The words of the blessing carry the power to control and direct the life of the person over whom they have been spoken. The Prophetic Blessing will revolutionize your life, and the lives of your children and grandchildren, to rise to a higher level of accomplishment, creating spiritual, physical, emotional, and relational prosperity" (Hagee, 2014).

Verbally speak out loud over your child's future the same thing (or something similar) as what Samuel's mom spoke over him. Prophesy over each of them.

In 1 Samuel 1:28 (NIV), it says, "'So now I give him to the LORD. For his whole life he will be given over to the LORD.' And he worshiped the LORD there."

When you declare your children's future, you are prophesying over them. What you declare with your mouth is important. Jesus says that you will have what you "say."

First, you need to have faith. What makes this message so revolutionary is now parents can be full of faith concerning how their children will turn out. Satan has tricked many parents into believing that children will either get saved or lost regardless of what the parent does. I'm sent by God to tell you to have faith in God that you can raise a child who will never smoke, never get drunk, never do drugs, never commit suicide, and never have sex outside of marriage and always love God. Yes, you can! You can raise a child similar to Tim Tebow, the 2007 Heisman Trophy winner, drafted to the Denver Broncos in the first round of 2010. I'm not saying your child will make it to the NFL. I'm not talking about having the same career but the same godly character.

We live in a society where parents, even Christian parents, have given up. Instead of handing down commandments, they are handing down condoms. Instead of teaching the Bible, they are teaching birth control. However, I do believe if we have not completely trained them in the way they should go and they choose to be sexually immoral, they should use a condom. Just as if our children were going to drive without a license, I believe they should still wear their seat belt. I also believe that if we start early enough, our children will choose not to drive until they have a license, because they desire to please God more than themselves, if you catch the analogy.

Most people do not prophesy over their children that they will be fully committed to the Lord their whole life. Many parents even in church speak contrary things over their children like, "You will have to learn the hard way," "You are stubborn like your father," "You are so hardheaded," and "You are so bad!" You should never speak things like this over your children.

On the contrary, what you should speak over them are things like, "You will be fully committed to the Lord all the days of your life. You will never get drunk or do drugs. You will never smoke, commit suicide, murder, or practice idolatry. You will never have sex outside of a God-ordained marriage, and you will marry a godly person that God has for you, in Jesus's name!" If this is what you desire for your children, declare this over them.

"Death and life are in the power of the tongue" (Proverbs 18:21a NKJV).

Look at these other people who had their future declared with prophecies over them and served the Lord from birth until burial.

Isaiah declared Mary (Jesus's mother) would be a virgin: "Therefore the Lord Himself will give you a sign: Behold, the virgin shall conceive and bear a Son, and shall call His name Immanuel" (Isaiah 7:14 NKJV).

The angel declared John the Baptist would have the Holy Spirit, bring them joy, and never drink wine.

> Do not be afraid, Zacharias, for your prayer is heard; and your wife Elizabeth will bear you a son, and you shall call his name John. And you will have joy and gladness, and many will rejoice at his birth. For he will be great in the sight of the Lord, and shall drink neither wine nor strong drink. He will also be filled with the Holy Spirit, even from his mother's womb. And he will turn many of the children of Israel to the Lord their God. He will also go before Him in the spirit

and power of Elijah, "to turn the hearts of the fathers to the children," and the disobedient to the wisdom of the just, to make ready a people prepared for the Lord. (Luke 1:13–16 NKJV)

Timothy had prophecies declared over him. "This charge I commit to you, son Timothy, according to the prophecies previously made concerning you, that by them you may wage the good warfare" (1 Timothy1:18 NKJV).

A man of God declared Josiah's future and spoke to the altar saying, "Behold, a child, Josiah by name, shall be born to the house of David; and on you he shall sacrifice the priests of the high places who burn incense on you, and men's bones shall be burned on you" (1 Kings 13:2b NKJV).

Finally, Jesus, our prime example, had this prophesied about His future:

> For unto us a Child is born,
> Unto us a Son is given;
> And the government will be upon His shoulder.
> And His name will be called
> Wonderful, Counselor, Mighty God,
> Everlasting Father, Prince of Peace. (Isaiah 9:6 NKJV).

This is just one of many. Never say to your children, "You are stupid," "You're a liar," or "You're a little devil," and so on. No matter what they do, or how bad it is, you should call them what you want them to be. If your children sneak and take a toy from their sibling, when you catch them, you don't say, "Give that back, you thief." If you do that, you are affirming them as a thief. In the same scenario, you can call them what you want them to be. "Give that back. You are not a thief. You are a good child." You still told them to give the item back, but now you have affirmed them as good children.

If your children run out of a room because it's dark, you don't say, "You're a chicken. Go back in there and turn the light on." Instead, you could say, "You are brave. Go back in and turn the lights on." When my three-year-old son came out of a dark room scared and I told him he was brave, my son immediately asked me, "Am I brave?" Then I repeated myself, "Yes, you're brave." I highly recommend the book *Hung by the Tongue* (1996) by Francis P. Martin. It goes into depth about the power of words. "The tongue has the power of life and death, and those who love it will eat its fruit" (Proverbs 18:21 NIV).

Naming Your Child

What you name your child matters.

Before you choose your child's name, you should seek God to find out if the Holy Spirit has a name for your child. Look up the meaning of a name before you consider it as an option. Do not make up your own meaning. Find out the origin of the name. Once you choose a name, you should pray for confirmation. The Lord will let you know if He rejects the name most likely by a check in your spirit. The reason a name is so important is because you will speak it over your child several times a day, every day, for the rest of his or her life. If the power of life and death is in what you say, you should want to speak something positive over your children rather than something negative. In 1 Samuel 25:25a (NKJV), it says, "Please, let not my lord regard this scoundrel Nabal. For as his name is, so is he: Nabal is his name, and folly is with him!" In Hebrew, the name Nabal means "fool."

A name is so important that God Himself has named children.

"Then God said, 'Yes, but your wife Sarah will bear you a son, and you will call him Isaac. I will establish my covenant with him as an everlasting covenant for his descendants after him'" (Genesis 17:19 NKJV). Isaac means "he laughs." Another example is John. "But the angel said to him: 'Do not be afraid, Zechariah; your prayer has been heard. Your wife Elizabeth will bear you a son, and you are to give him the name John'" (Luke 1:13 NKJV). John means "The Lord is gracious." Even though the name *Isaac* does not seem to be spiritual, the point is your child's name is important and you should not call your child something that has a negative meaning.

God lets us know that a name is so important that He changed many individuals' names in the Bible.

- Abram (meaning "exalted father") to Abraham (meaning "father of many nations") (Genesis 17:5)
- Sarai to Sarah (both names mean "princess") (Genesis 17:15) "But now she was to be the mother of many nations set apart for God's purpose" (verse 16).
- Jacob (meaning "supplanter"—to take the place of another, as through force, scheming, strategy, or the like) was changed to Israel (meaning "he struggles with God" (Genesis 32:28).

After you pick a name, then it is important to call your child by that name. If you create a nickname for that child, then you should know what the nickname means. Don't call the child something that you don't want him or her to be. Don't call your child a devil or "trouble." Choose a nickname carefully if that is what you are going to speak over your child. A nickname can be as important as the actual name, if that is what you are going to call your child.

If you don't think a name or nickname is important, ask Jesus what He thinks. Jesus gave a nickname to some of His disciples. "James son of Zebedee and his brother John (to them he gave the name Boanerges, which means Sons of Thunder)" (Mark 3:17 NIV). Jesus said to Simon Peter, "Blessed art thou, Simon Barjona: for flesh and blood hath not revealed it unto thee, but my Father which is in heaven. And I say also unto thee, that thou art Peter, and upon this rock I will build my church; and the gates of hell shall not prevail against it" (Matthew 16:17–18 KJV). *Peter* means "stone."

This is only one step in the process of producing a child who will be committed to the Lord all his or her life. The name alone will not cause your child to be saved or lost. I had the pleasure of doing stand-up comedy and touring with the legendary comedian Sinbad. Using the name, "Sin Bad" did not stop him from being a Christian. He is a Christian who chose the name because of his admiration of Sinbad the Sailor.

You can choose a name based on the life of someone else you esteem. The child may take on the qualities of that person. We named our daughter Jael, after the Jael of the Bible. "Most blessed among women is Jael" (Judges 5:24a NKJV). She killed the leader of the army who fought against Israel by driving a tent peg through his skull with a hammer. It's no wonder that our daughter is what most would consider a tomboy.

If a child's first name is Hell and his or her last name is Bound, that does not mean that child is bound to go to hell. The same rule applies if his or her first name is heaven. It does not mean that he or she automatically will go to heaven. There are still many other factors involved (although if my first name was "Hell," I would change it at the first opportunity). If you find your child has a name with a negative meaning, you can change it or choose a different nickname to call him or her.

Be careful of word curses from people who will speak against your words of blessing. If you say out loud, "My children are going to be a blessing to me when they are teenagers." Those who have not experienced that may send out word curses and say something like, "No, they won't. Your teenagers will be rebellious just like everyone else's," or "You think it's rough when your children are babies; they will be much worse when they are teenagers." You will find this happens far too often in our churches. Do not be surprised or discouraged when it comes from pastors, elders, or other members of the clergy. They may think you are naïve and ignorant, so they are preparing you for the worst. Unfortunately, many Christians are only subject to their own experiences. Therefore, if they have had an extremely rough time with their teenagers, they may be unaware when they try to speak word curses on your kids.

I have seen teenagers who are fully committed to the Lord and are a true blessing to their parents. You need to speak that your children will be included in that minority and don't receive anything else. When someone says something like, "Your child is going to be just as bad as you were when you were a teenager," you should say (silently if necessary), "I don't receive that. My child will be better than I was." Even Jesus himself said, "Most assuredly, I say to you, he who believes in Me, the works that I do he will do also; and greater works than these he will do, because I go to My Father" (John 14:12 NKJV). If Jesus can speak that the next generation can do greater things than He did, we can confidently speak that our children will do greater things than we have done.

We received a Christian baby book as a present for our first baby shower. It was awesome. Instead of saying "the terrible twos," there was a page titled, "The Terrific Twos." Even though we had many moments that were not so terrific, we still spoke of the time period as the "terrific twos" for all our children. James 3:1–12 describes the power of the tongue. According to verse 6, the tongue sets on fire the course of our life.

During the ceremony when you dedicate your child to God is an excellent time to declare over your child the prophetic blessing. You can also do it at other times, at home, or start when your child is in the womb. We need to declare what we want our children to be.

In order to guarantee your child will serve the Lord all the days of his or her life and go to heaven, you need to declare it!

Chapter 10

Receive Resources on
Family Regularly

My people are destroyed for lack of knowledge. Because
you have rejected knowledge, I also will reject you from
being priest for Me; Because you have forgotten the
law of your God, I also will forget your children.
—Hosea 4:6 (NKJV)

Previous generations had the excuse that they may not have
known what to do as a husband, wife, father, or mother, because
they may not have had an example to follow or resources to
teach them. We have all heard the phrase, "They did the best they …
could." Some of you may be thinking, *No, my parent could have done
better.* That may be true, but take a moment and think about what
example they had and what resources they had access to.

Until now, God did not blame the parents for the errors of their children.

Ezekiel 18:20 (NIV) says, "The one who sins is the one who will die. The
child will not share the guilt of the parent, nor will the parent share the
guilt of the child. The righteousness of the righteous will be credited to
them, and the wickedness of the wicked will be charged against them."

Our Old Testament heroes did not have the knowledge or the help we
have today. They did not have the Holy Spirit, Jesus's living example,

or the New Testament scriptures. Even in the New Testament times, no one had access to the completed New Testament. In addition, our ancestors did not have access to excellent resources around the world twenty-four hours a day, seven days a week as we do.

But now, we no longer have the excuse of ignorance. God has poured out the knowledge in resources, and there are more resources available now for the body of Christ than ever before in history. The resources have been available for a significant amount of time now; however, this book is revealing that now God requires us to seek these resources out. We will be held accountable for not knowing how to be a godly spouse or parent.

There is a shift in the responsibilities of the Christian parent.

Acts 17:30 (NIV) says, "In the past God overlooked such ignorance, but now he commands all people everywhere to repent."

In other words, God did not blame our parents for their children rejecting the truth, but He will be blaming us in our generation for our children rejecting the truth. If we do not train them properly, it will be our fault; either we did not find out how to be the parent God wanted us to be, or we did not choose to be the parent God wanted us to be.

If we are married, we must use resources on marriage. If we are a parent, we must use resources on parenting. What do I mean by resources? Books, audiobooks, e-books, online content, seminars, trainings, and teachings (live or recorded on the latest recording devices), and the list goes on.

We need to go through one book, one seminar, or one training a year on parenting. If we are married, we need to go through one book, seminar, or training on marriage per year. Many professions have what's called "continuing education."

When I was a mortgage broker, every year, we had to go through four hours of training in order to keep our license. This gave us new information and reminded us of previous information in order to continue to do our job well.

What if our marriage license worked the same way? What if we did not go through marriage education classes every year, the government would cause us to lose our marriage license? The reality is about half the people who get a marriage license will lose it in divorce (if they get married at all). However, those who willingly submit to quality relationship education not only stay married longer but stay "happily married." Who wants to be miserably married for fifty years just so they can say they've been married for fifty years? Not me!

Unfortunately, many people have been trained to accept advice from a pulpit or an individual but reject the same advice if it comes from a book. The mentality is "You can't learn how to be a good spouse or parent from a book." However, God chose to use books for thousands of years to teach us. God never stopped using books. In the past, it was illegal for Black Americans to read or even to help them read. There is a spirit that tries to prevent Black Americans and all cultures from reading, especially from reading the books of the Bible. It has resulted in a reluctant attitude toward reading. May God break that stronghold and give us a hunger and thirst for godly knowledge.

I recommend reading *The Five Love Languages* by Dr. Gary Chapman, as mentioned earlier. We need to know the five love languages just as we know the five senses. This information alone has helped millions have more successful relationships and can help millions more.

You should start with the resource that is most relevant to your situation. Let the Holy Spirit guide you. Depending on your circumstances, you may start with *The Five Love Languages of Children*, *The Five Love Languages of Teenagers*, or *Parenting Your Adult Child* by Dr. Chapman.

I recommended the following books by Dr. James Dobson also, considered the leading teacher on parenting in the United States:

Bringing Up Boys if you have a boy and *Bringing Up Girls* if you have a girl. While reading these books, I went from being interested in my kids' schoolwork to being involved in my kids' schoolwork. Interested says "Did you do your work?" Involved says, "Let me help you with it." These books and many others have changed countless lives and families for the better. Our life has been changed by my pastors Stephen and Yolanda Fairfax, who were the first to introduce me to my family mentors Dr. Chapman and Dr. Dobson.

Luke 12:47–48 (NKJV) says, "And that servant who knew his master's will, and did not prepare himself or do according to his will, shall be beaten with many stripes. But he who did not know, yet committed things deserving of stripes, shall be beaten with few. For everyone to whom much is given, from him much will be required; and to whom much has been committed, of him they will ask the more."

On one hand, it is wonderful to be given more knowledge of God's will and understanding of His plans than any previous generation. On the other hand, that means that more is required of this generation than any generation before.

For example, let's say you did not give your children daily bread because you did not know that it was required of you. The good news is now you know one thing that is going to cause your children to love God and be more like Jesus. At the same time, if you still decide not to give your children their daily bread for whatever reason, you will open your family up to the enemy even more, and you will be worse off than if you never knew. So I sincerely hope you receive the good news and apply it.

God is now blaming the new parents more than any previous generation because many parents are just now finding out what their parental responsibilities are. He is using this book and many other teachers and preachers to get the message out. God has sent too many teachers with more than enough resources to teach His people how to be the parents He has called them to be. If you choose to reject God's teachers, then you are rejecting God and you and your children will suffer because of the knowledge you rejected. Listen to Hosea 4:6 (NKJV) again. God says,

> My people are destroyed for lack of knowledge.
> Because you have rejected knowledge,
> I also will reject you from being priest for Me;
> Because you have forgotten the law of your God,
> I also will forget your children.

If God has called your pastor to write books, then He has also called the congregation to read the books. The whole body of Christ should regularly be receiving the information God is sending through books, whether e-books, books on CD, or websites through your cell phone, tablet, laptop, or the latest devices, which are constantly coming out. Not having any money is no excuse. Dr. James Dobson and others even have phenomenal information shared on YouTube for free or you may get a free library card. We will make time for what we believe is important. Pastor Stephen E. Fairfax says, "Excuses only please the one who makes them."

We now have teachers, pastors, evangelists, prophets, and apostles. The full five-fold ministry is in operation. God has called them to write, and He is requiring His people to read. The library section on Christian living is flooded. He does not want His people destroyed for lack of knowledge. I heard the saying, "What you don't know won't hurt you," but the truth is what you don't know could kill you.

Many of the men in our previous generations thought their only job was to provide financially. They did not know that a man's job is to provide spiritually, physically, emotionally (mentally), relationally (socially), and financially. By the end of this book, you will be able to identify exactly what you need to do as a parent to guarantee your children go to heaven. Then it is up to you.

Now for the first time in history, God is putting the responsibility on the parents. I am not saying you are accountable for what you did not know in the past; I am saying you are accountable now for what you do know going forward.

"The righteousness of the righteous shall be upon himself, and the wickedness of the wicked shall be upon himself" (Ezekiel 18:20b NKJV). Therefore, if parents now know that God requires them to give their children daily bread and now know that letting the children go a week without feeding them spiritually can cause them to die spiritually, wouldn't it be wicked for the parents to let their children starve? What would a righteous parent do? Now that we know this principle, let's choose to be righteous parents.

For the most part, God did not blame the previous generations, from our parents all the way back to Bible times. He did not blame David or Samuel around 1000 BC for their bad children or Jacob around 1900 BC for his bad kids. We do not have a record of God blaming Adam and Eve for their eldest child murdering his brother.

God did correct Eli the priest for not disciplining his children, and that was only when Eli's kids already had "no regard for the Lord" (1 Samuel 2:12 NIV). Even though God did not blame the previous generations for their parenting for the most part, God has told me to preach, "In the past God overlooked such ignorance, but now he commands all people everywhere to repent" (Acts 17:30 NIV). God will hold us accountable if we do not do the parenting job He has called us to do when it is well within our power to get the knowledge and do it.

In order for us to guarantee our children go to heaven, we must receive the resources on Christian parenting, marriage, and family. Receive does not just mean purchase them; it means to do what God says through whatever teaching we hear or read. We must receive them into our homes and, most important, into our hearts.

And this I pray, that your love may abound more and more [displaying itself in greater depth] in real knowledge and in practical insight, so that you may learn to recognize and treasure what is excellent [identifying the best, and distinguishing moral differences], and that you may be pure and blameless until the day of Christ [actually living lives that lead others away from sin]. (Philippians 1:9–10 AMP)

Chapter 11

Esteem and Love Your
Children Properly

He (Jesus) replied, "It is not right to take the
children's bread and toss it to the dogs."
—Matthew 15:26 (NIV)

How is it that so many parents say they love their children, yet
so many children say they don't feel loved? It is because too
many parents are not prioritizing their children and speaking
the love language of their child, as mentioned before. The saying is true
for how children feel about their parents—"They don't care how much
you know until they know how much you care."

Do not put the church, work, extended family, or others before your
own children. Make sure your children get enough time with you. Make
sure they feel loved by speaking their love language.

The order of God was ordained from the beginning. Before marriage,
He created a relationship between God and man and then between
man and woman in marriage; next was children and afterward extended
family and others. Our priorities should be demonstrated in the order
God created—God first, because we should have a relationship with
Him first; then our spouse should come next; then our children. After
the family comes the church. That's right; contrary to popular view,
your immediate family should come before the church family (unless

you are a single adult). Since the beginning, "God's family and creating a godly family, was near and dear to God's heart … Almost every problem we see today is a result of family problems and issues" (Keesee, 2015, 80).

In the past, we were taught to put God first. However, we were taught in error that putting God first means putting the church first; therefore, clergy and church members neglected their spouse's needs and their children's needs to do "church work." We spent time with our choir when we should have spent time with our kids. We were there for the service when we should have been there for our spouse. We were trying to save souls in the house of God when we first should have been saving the souls in our own house.

> But if a widow has children or grandchildren, these should learn first of all to put their religion into practice by caring for their own family and so repaying their parents and grandparents, for this is pleasing to God. … Anyone who does not provide for their relatives, and especially for their own household, has denied the faith and is worse than an unbeliever. (1 Timothy 5:4, 8 NIV)

Chapter 12

Never Let Them Stay under Ungodly Influence

Blessed is the man who walks not in the counsel of the ungodly, Nor stands in the path of sinners, Nor sits in the seat of the scornful; But his delight is in the law of the LORD, And in His law he meditates day and night. He shall be like a tree planted by the rivers of water, That brings forth its fruit in its season, Whose leaf also shall not wither; And whatever he does shall prosper.
—Psalm 1:1–3 (NKJV)

D id you hear that promise? If you do this, your child's "leaf shall never wither." That means never die spiritually. Parents have two main responsibilities: sow good seeds and keep out weeds.

"And some seed fell among thorns; and the thorns grew up and choked it, and it yielded no crop." (Mark 4:7 NKJV).

Not only are we responsible for the seeds we sow in our children, we are responsible for all the weeds that are sown in our children. Weeds can be referred to as bad seeds or thorns. I am not saying that every weed sown is our fault; I'm saying every weed is our responsibility.

"Now these are the ones sown among thorns; they are the ones who hear the word, and the cares of this world, the deceitfulness of riches, and the desires for other things entering in choke the word, and it becomes unfruitful" (Mark 4:18–19 NKJV).

We have a responsibility to make sure our six-year-old children are not watching PG-13 or R-rated movies and programs (this includes rated T (teen) and M (mature) video games), listening to PA (parental advisory) music, looking at inappropriate things on the Internet, and so on. All these things are weeds that the world is trying to sow into our children. If we let them take root, they will choke the good seeds that have been planted. It's been said we need to get to the root of the problem! But I say we need to get to the seed of the problem before it takes root!

I was at a boys' and men's retreat, talking with and listening to teenagers. They said that they knew girls and guys who went wild (pursued sex, drinking, drugs, and the party life) when they left their parents' house, because their parents were too strict. I explained to them that often people think if you give your children strict rules, they will do everything you did not allow them to do as soon as they leave your home or even leave your presence. This happens when parents allow their children to receive and grow bad seeds in their hearts, and then they try to put strict rules on the fruit of those seeds. This is a bad plan that often ends with a lot of conflict between parent and child.

Children will desire what they experience, see, and hear. They don't know what they don't know. How can they say they like a song they have never heard or a movie they have never experienced? If parents focus on what their kids see and hear, then they can help control their kids' likes and desires.

Parents often don't stop their kids from listening to SADDDDD music. This is music that promotes selfishness, adultery (sexual lust—"Whoever looks at a woman to lust for her has already committed adultery with her in his heart" (Matthew 5:28 NKJV)), drunkenness, drugs, degrading women, deceitful riches, and destructive violence. If your children regularly listen to that music, don't be surprised when they desire to drink, practice sexual immorality, do drugs, commit violence, or not value women and girls. Even females are not valuing themselves as a result of this music.

It's sad when the unaware parents who let their children listen to this music every day try to set rules to prevent their children from doing all these things. They tell the children it is against their rules. Well, if something is against your rules don't let your children desire it. Don't only make it against the rules for your children to have sex outside of marriage, make it against your rules to listen to or watch things that promote sex outside marriage.

We must get to the seed of the problem before it takes root! At eleven years of age, my son received a ride from a family member he does not often see. The family member started playing the popular SADDDDD music he and his children normally listen to. My son spoke up. He said, "I'm not allowed to listen to this music."

The family member had no problem quickly turning the station to Christian music that they all liked. I was nowhere around, and my son did not have to speak up. He could have just sat there and said nothing, and I would have never known. I found out because my son was excited to tell me.

When my son was out of my presence, he stood up for what he was taught, and he wanted to please me even when I was not around. He was proud to tell me the story, and I was overjoyed to hear it. My wife and I never allowed him to listen to SADDDDD music, and as a result, he has no desire to listen to it. He desires positive music that promotes God. Music is so powerful because it is Satan's number-one weapon. God created Lucifer to excel in music before he turned into Satan and used it for evil.

"The workmanship of your timbrels and pipes was prepared for you on the day you were created" (Ezekiel 28:13b NKJV).

Marketers understand the power of music. They pay thousands of dollars for songs to be added to their commercials to get their message across. Some may think that all they listen to is the beat of the music. But even if our kids just listen to the beat, the message from the music is what is being sown into them.

This is why I never let my daughter listen to Beyoncé or other musical artists who have a spirit of lust. Beyoncé was named by *Time* magazine as one of the one hundred most influential people in the world and was featured on their cover of May 12, 2014. I understand her influence on the world but not in the church. We cannot allow our children to be seduced by this music promoting lust and sex at a young age. We should do everything in our power to make sure they don't hear it.

Listening to this type of music opens us up to receive evil spirits. Beyoncé admits that she is possessed by a spirit named Sasha Fierce. When people go to her concerts, they are being entertained by a spirit named Sasha Fierce who tries to seduce many into sexual sin. Beyoncé explained that Sasha takes over when she is doing a video and when she is onstage. Beyoncé says, "When I see a video of myself or on TV I'm like, who's that girl that's not me. I wouldn't dare do that. I turn into Sasha. I wouldn't like Sasha if I met her offstage. She's too aggressive, too strong, too sassy, too sexy! I'm not like her in real life at all. I'm not flirtatious and superconfident and fearless like her" (Thompson, 2008).

She also said, "What I feel onstage I don't feel anywhere else. It's an out-of-body experience. I created my stage persona ... so that when I go home, I don't have to think about what it is I do. Sasha isn't me" (Thompson, 2008).

Beyoncé performs as Sasha, yet she does not like Sasha. At the same time, we should not like Sasha either, nor should we allow our children to be entertained by a spirit. We must not forget that a third of Jesus's ministry involved Him casting out spirits (demons). "Then He healed many who were sick with various diseases, and cast out many demons" (Mark 1:34a NKJV).

We may need to cast an evil spirit out of our children. If you are not sure if your child has one, pray and let the Holy Spirit reveal it to you. Either way, if you have God's Spirit in you, you have the authority to say to your child, "I command any and every evil spirit to come out in the name of the Lord Jesus Christ!"

Not every secular artist has an evil spirit or even has a negative message. The problem comes when our children listen to a secular artist so much that they become in love with the artist and accept anything that the artist produces. Therefore, when the artist produces SADDDDD music, our children receive that message also.

Our children are even being seduced into worshiping these artists. The show *American Idol* had a fitting title because the popstars become idols, loved and worshipped by fans who get enthralled by them. They give their offerings at the concerts with the purchase of their tickets; they lift their hands and dance to a message that often demands worship.

Beyoncé's husband, Jay-Z, calls himself J Hova as in Jehovah God's name (Exodus 6:3) and tells others to lift their hands to him. "H' to the (izz) O, V to the (izz), 'A' that's the anthem, get your d**n hands up!" (Jay-Z, 2001) is the hook to his song "Izzo (H.O.V.A.)" produced by Kanye West.

If we let our children continually listen to this type of music, they could worship these "American idols" and, most important, their hearts will be turned away from the true Jehovah, our God.

Another example is Justin Bieber. As Christ followers, we are called believers. Justin Bieber's followers are called "Beliebers." If you do not want your son or daughter involved in a relationship too early or involved in sex before they are married, you should not let them listen to the message in his negative music (or any other music that promotes early relationships before people are ready for marriage). This is from Justin Bieber's song "All That Matters" (2014):

Take the gas out the car it won't drive,
That's how I feel when you're not by my side,
When I wake up in the morning up under you, and only you.

When our children begin to love these artists and this secular music, in many cases, serving God and being included in the praise and worship of God will not be important to them, and they will not know why. It is because the Word has been choked by this music. As a result, our children often couldn't care less if they came to church. And if they do come, it will often be for observation instead of participation in worshiping God in spirit and truth. "But the hour is coming, and now is, when the true worshipers will worship the Father in spirit and truth; for the Father is seeking such to worship Him. God is Spirit, and those who worship Him must worship in spirit and truth" (John 4:23–24 NKJV).

So when you hear your child listening to music, find out what the message is, what the title of the song is, and who it is by. Don't allow the enemy to steal the hearts of your children through music. Don't allow him to whisper in their ear with headphones so you cannot hear their words or protect them.

"For by your words you will be justified, and by your words you will be condemned" (Matthew 5:37 NKJV).

People often judge music by the beat, but if we want to follow God's way, we will judge by the words. We should not be quick to condemn or approve music simply off of the beat but the message (if there is one).

Sometimes we promote the negative message unconsciously. Christians are too often unaware that they are financially supporting the same artists who are negatively influencing our youth by buying and wearing their clothes. Years ago, I stopped wearing clothes like "Sean John" by Sean "Puffy" Combs and RocaWear by Jay-Z. These artists often make more money from the clothing sales than music sales. We can put that same financial support toward Christian clothing like 116 Clique by Lecrae or God Over Money by Bizzle, familychristian.com, and other artists who positively influence our youth with their message.

Check the ratings of all your children's music as well as movies, video games, TV shows, websites, and so on. If it is PG-13 or rated teen because of sexual content or language, don't allow your children to watch or listen to it. If you think something is questionable, review it first before you allow your children to see or listen to it.

My son was seven years old and was having a hard time understanding why almost all his friends, including his church friends and family, had seen the movie *Transformers* rated PG-13. He knew he was not allowed to see it because he was only seven; however, many of his friends and family were younger than he was and they had all seen it. I told him not to fall into the trap that Adam and Eve did; they focused on the tree they could not eat instead of all the ones they could.

Our children have too many positive alternatives to allow them to look at and listen to the media outlets they are not old enough for. I like Sponge Bob, Superbook, Dora, and Veggie Tales. We just have to look.

Pure Flix is a faith-based family entertainment subscription that can be used for our families to have a good time together and get a good message. It is full of great movies, shows, documentaries, and educational materials. I recommend it for all kids in school or homeschool. I don't believe the answer for our children is just to keep them away from the media and internet but to use the media and internet as tools to positively influence our children.

Do not let them have media or technology that is not appropriate for their age. As a general rule, don't let them view PG-13 (or worse) movies before they are thirteen. Preview the movies and content first. Ask yourself, "What message is this sending to my kids?" Do not let movies cause your children to desire the occult, relationships to early, or anything else you don't want them involved in. It's also important to note that just because it may be rated age appropriate does not mean it's automatically okay to see. The ratings are becoming more and more lax; investigate it first. The Bible says to "avoid godless chatter, because those who indulge in it will become more and more ungodly" (2 Timothy 2:16 NIV).

Choose your children's friends and the family they hang around wisely. They will be friends with the kids and family members whom you allow them to associate with. I hope you have a church or family community that will be in agreement with you. Then your kids will be a positive influence on their kids, and their kids will be a positive influence on your kids. It is not good for your children to receive a lot of socialization if those they socialize with are going to introduce them to a lot of the negative things you are trying to protect them from.

Consider this situation. You would never let your children look at pornography (a child viewing this is a form of sexual abuse), but other children view it often with no parent around to stop them. What do you think these children will want to tell your children about? The saying goes, "It takes a village to raise a child," and we need parents who have similar values for our children to be raised in a healthier environment. You may want to go through this book as a group to get other parents on the same page.

This book is mainly about starting early and preventing our children from leaving Christ; however, if they have already been entangled in the web of secular music, you can still help them break free. Apologize for not holding a standard in the past and let them know that from now on you want to sow positive seeds into them and give them a message that God agrees with instead of one that is being used to destroy them. Then give them alternative music and artists they will enjoy that promote Christ and positive things. I like gospel music. My wife and I like Hillsong and Christian rap. Our eleven-year-old son likes Lecrae (although we still judge his music by the message). Our ten-year-old daughter likes Jamie Grace, and our four-year-old likes the whole 116 Clique (just to name a few we like). Once you find a song you like, many music services, like Amazon, give suggested songs and artists you may also enjoy.

If you purposely only expose your children to Christian music starting off, they will love it regardless of whatever genre of Christian music they are into. Don't judge the music by the beat; judge the music by the message.

> But those things which proceed out of the mouth come from the heart, and they defile a man. For out of the heart proceed evil thoughts, murders, adulteries, fornications, thefts, false witness, blasphemies. These are the things which defile a man. (Matthew 15:18–20a NKJV).

The same thing goes for TV shows, videos, movies, video games, and so on. As our children are exposed to these media outlets, it is imperative that they are age appropriate. One of the hardest sacrifices we face as parents is not watching movies around our children that they are not ready for.

As parents, the PG-13 Marvel movie may be fine for us but not for our five-year-old child. There was a man who went to our church and wanted to do something nice for several of the young people. So he took them to see a Batman movie. The problem was they were between five and seven years of age, and the Batman movie was rated PG-13. These movies often promote sex outside of marriage, as we see Bruce Wayne waking up in bed with his latest girlfriend. We too often don't recognize the message that we are allowing to be planted in our children. Do not allow the movies to send messages that choke the word of God from our children.

Video games are fun! They can be positive and constructive or negative and destructive or even addicting. The good thing is they are also rated for us parents who may not have the time or energy to investigate every video game that comes out. Simply go with the ratings on the front. If your child is old enough to play it, then investigate it. In this case, it is beneficial to "judge a book by its cover." The ratings are set by the ESRB (Entertainment Software Rating Board, www.esrb.org).

This general knowledge about the ratings are my own summaries. They mainly come from my own experience playing video games, as well as information from www.esrb.org and www.commensemedia.org. You will typically see the ratings right on the front of the games with a letter to represent the rating. "E" stands for "everyone," which means it is typically appropriate for all ages. "E" with a small "10" on it is typically appropriate for ages ten and up. It may have mild language or a small amount of suggestive themes.

Rated "T" is typically appropriate for teenagers, thirteen or older. It may have some profanity, violence, blood, or suggestive themes. The next highest rating you will see is "M." This stands for "mature." These games are intended to be for ages seventeen and older. It could contain sexual content, extreme violence, blood and gore, and strong profanity.

Finally, an "A" rating stands for "adults," ages eighteen and older. These games may contain a lot of extreme violence, gambling with real money, or explicit sexual content in addition to the things mentioned in previous ratings.

You can get a more detailed analysis from www.commonsensemedia. org, which describes why each video game is rated the way it is rated. They are a great resource. Their website states, "Common Sense Media helps families make smart media choices. We offer the largest, most trusted library of independent age-based and educational ratings and reviews for movies, games, apps, TV shows, websites, books, and music" (Commonsense Media, 2016).

Many parents are asking the question, "Is my child mature enough to play (or watch) this game that is rated over their age?" But this is the wrong question. A better question is, "Are there plenty of games (or shows) they can be entertained by that are appropriate for their age?" And the answer to that is a profound "Yes!" You also teach them patience when they must wait for the age-appropriate game.

At the same time, we should not allow our children to spend a lot of time in these media outlets daily. It can cause them to be unhealthy, self-centered, or lack motivation to do anything. The American Academy of Pediatrics (AAP) recommends parents avoid television viewing and screen time for children under the age of two.

> The AAP believe the negative effects of media use far outweigh the positive ones for this age group. Despite the luminous claims of educational videos and software, little evidence supports educational or developmental benefits from media use by children younger than 2 years. Researchers examined twelve-, twenty-four-, and thirty-six-month-olds and found that background television not only reduced the length of time a child played, but it also reduced the child's focused attention during play. (Chapman and Pellicane, 2014).

Since there are so many different uses and categories of screen time, it is hard to put a specific recommendation on how much "screen time" is appropriate. The most important thing is that you pay attention to what is being done on screen time. Continue to follow the leading of the Holy Spirit. If you feel that your children are spending too much time playing video games, on the Internet, on their device, or watching TV, they probably are. You must give children activities to keep them balanced. "Be wise as serpents and harmless as doves" (Matthew 10:16b NKJV).

Require reading time daily. According to www.k12reader.com, it is critical to include twenty minutes of reading in your child's daily schedule. Reading improves brain development, literacy skills, and listening skills. And don't we all want our children to listen more? Make them read (www.k12reader.com, 2016).

This twenty minutes of reading is in addition to school. This should also include some minutes in the age-appropriate Bible. Ask your children, grandchildren, nieces, or nephews, "Have you spent your twenty minutes reading today?" Do not let them just sit and play video games (or other idle activities) on your watch. This reading requirement will set your children up to be successful in education.

Also make sure your children are exercising daily. This is the recommended time for children to be active set by the National Health Service (www.nhs.uk).

Children under Five

Children under five who can walk unaided should be physically active every day for at least 180 minutes (three hours), spread throughout the day, indoors or out.

If your children are under five, you should encourage them to do light activity and more energetic physical activity.

Children and Young People Aged Five to Eighteen

Children and young people aged five to eighteen should do at least sixty minutes (one hour) of aerobic activity every day. This should include a mix of moderate-intensity activities, which means they are working hard enough to raise their heart rate and break a sweat, and vigorous-intensity activities, which means they're breathing hard and fast and their heart rate has gone up quite a bit.

As part of your children's sixty or more minutes, they should also do activities that strengthen their muscles and bones (nhs.uk, 2016).

Find a sport they like. It could be basketball, football, baseball, or a slew of others, including gymnastics, dance, or martial arts. If they are part of a team, they should have regular practice, and even when they don't, you can have them practice at home, or, even better, you could practice with them. When my son was eleven, I would challenge him to a push-up competition with my three-year-old on my back. They both loved it!

Sometimes children seem not to like any sport. This was the case with my godson Julian. However, when he got a hold of the video game *Dance Dance Revolution 3* on the Nintendo Wii (or Wii U), he enjoyed working out on it for hours (avoiding the songs with negative messages). Even though the Wii came out in 2006, he bought it in 2016 and is having a blast. The Wii has many games that can make working out and family time a lot of fun. Sometimes the latest system is not the greatest system.

Reading, exercising, entertainment, God's Word, prayer, helping the needy, and being productive need to be balanced in our lives and in the lives of our children. This prevents weeds from creeping into their lives and choking the Word of God.

Do not let your children go to a worldly public school in elementary. Children are highly influenced by their peers and teachers at this age more than ever. Often public schools have negative influences beginning from the time the kids get on the bus and hear the popular SADDDDD music. Christian schools and homeschooling (including schools online) are ways we can guarantee our children are learning without being flooded with negative and deceitful messages (more on this in chapter 15).

The counsel of the ungodly definitely includes babysitters, older cousins and family members, and everyone you bring into your home and allow around your children. We can learn a lot from the Good Samaritan.

Think about this. The Good Samaritan obviously had money and most likely had a very nice home. Why didn't he take the beaten person into his own home? I submit to you that he had a family, and even though he was helping someone, he put the person he was helping in a hotel so that his own family would be out of harm's way.

"He went to him and bandaged his wounds, pouring on oil and wine. Then he put the man on his own donkey, brought him to an inn, and took care of him. The next day, he took out two denarii and gave them to the innkeeper. "Look after him,' he said, 'and when I return, I will reimburse you for any extra expense you may have'" (Luke 10:34–35 NIV). In verse 37, Jesus said, "Go and do likewise."

When we help others, we must first make sure our own family is protected and taken care of. They are our first assignment. We should be careful whom we bring into our home when we want to show hospitality, as many Christians show. We cannot allow those we help to hurt our children or be more of a negative influence than a positive one.

When I was growing up, my mother was very hospitable. She would let distant family and others live with us from time to time. They were often older than I was and male. Without my dad in the home, I looked up to them automatically without knowing why. Although sometimes they helped me by taking me to school or practice, they also gave me bad advice and were a negative influence.

I believe if we would have had family devotions every night, their words and actions would not have had such an impact on me. I would have been washed in the Word daily so their stuff would not stick. In addition, my older cousins would have been influenced by the Word of God each night. It is very likely they would have been more conscious not to corrupt my brother and me to pursue sex and things at a young age.

I am not saying not to bring anyone who is not saved, sanctified, and fire baptized into your home. I'm saying be careful, like the Good Samaritan. He helped others and protected his family.

My wife and I were led by the Spirit to bring a youth into our home. To protect his identity, we will call the youth "John." John was on probation, involved with drugs, and flunking out of high school. We put him in a Christian school and negotiated for him to come to the football practice because his grades were too bad to play. We monitored his friends and, of course, we had devotions every night. He did not even notice he did not have time for TV much because each night after homework, we would read the scriptures and talk about what it meant to us, what it meant to him, and our mistakes and victories. As a result, he began to share his mistakes and victories.

We had a son in kindergarten and a four-year-old daughter at the time. We did not want him to feel like a babysitter, so we made sure our children were not left alone with him.

It was one of the hardest things we have ever done. The problems we encountered with John could be a whole book by itself. Yet, he respected our standard, and he even protected our children, making sure they did not see bad things or listen to the music he liked to listen to.

He stayed with us a year. The Holy Spirit worked on him powerfully. We went through the book *The Five Love Languages of Teenagers*, which really helped. Death had a contract on his life, but it was defeated! Thank you, Jesus! He went on to graduate high school and get a job. All glory to God!

If you never let your children stay under ungodly influence, you can have children fully committed to the Lord from birth until burial.

Part III

You Can Guarantee Their Salvation

Chapter 13

The Problem with The Purpose Driven Life

"Nevertheless I have this against you"
-Revelation 2:4a (NKJV)

Since 2007, the number-one Christian book sold in the United States was *The Purpose Driven Life* by Pastor Rick Warren. I received great revelation from the book; however, there is a major problem with one of the principles, which is detrimental to the body of Christ. As God spoke good things to the church of Ephesus, he also said, "Nevertheless I have this against you" (Revelation 2:4a NKJV). I believe God has something against *The Purpose Driven Life* book. The problem is the book teaches the body of Christ to put the church before their families, which is a proven error in traditional theology with grave consequences.

The author of the book is Pastor Rick Warren, the pastor of Saddleback Church. He did the inaugural prayer for the president in 2008. Pastor Warren and *The Purpose Driven Life* have been a tremendous blessing to me and my whole church in many areas. I have preached several messages from the book. My life was enriched after taking the forty-day journey through the pages.

Even though *The Purpose Driven Life* has been such an asset to me, I have not been able to truly recommend it to others and here is why. A message in the book has destroyed many Christian families. Throughout the book and specifically in Purpose # 2, Pastor Warren teaches, "God commands us to love the church as much as Jesus does" (Warren 2002). He tells us to give our life for the church. But this is a misquotation of Ephesians 5:25.

The Bible says God commands us to love our spouse as much as Jesus loved the church. Ephesians 5:25 (NKJV) says, "Husbands, love your wives, just as Christ also loved the church and gave Himself for her." God has called me and many others to teach that He does not want husbands to give their lives for the church. God tells husbands to give their lives for their wives.

Pastor Warren also taught in the book,

> The church is your spiritual family ... Your spiritual family is even more important than your physical family because it will last forever. Our families on earth are wonderful gifts from God, but they are temporary and fragile, often broken by divorce, distance, growing old and inevitably, death. On the other hand, our spiritual family—our relationship to other believers—will continue throughout eternity. It is a much stronger union, a more permanent bond, than blood relationships. (Warren 2002, 118)

He repeats in bold, italicized letters by itself on page 119, "Your spiritual family is even more important than your physical family."

Unfortunately, what he failed to teach is that your wife and children are your most important spiritual family, or at least they should be. Too many of our Christian families have suffered family devastation because we have been taught in error to prioritize the church family before our own spouse and children. Too many preachers have lost their marriages and too many pastors have lost their children as a result. The truth is

"Our marriage should come first. Next to our personal relationship with God, our marriage and family should be our top priority. Our ministry should flow out of the family," according to Pastor Gary Keesee, host of the TV show *Fixing the Money Thing* and senior pastor of Faith Life Church. The church must have this order correct in order to prosper the way God intended.

Pastor and evangelist Benny Henn explains the reason for his divorce in *Charisma News* on October 24, 2013, saying, "In my case, it was family and the stress of ministry and being too busy. I didn't pay attention to Suzanne's pain. That's what caused our problem." He has since corrected the error and has reconciled with his wife. Glory to God!

I love the way it was so eloquently explained by Dr. David Jeremiah, the pastor of Shadow Mountain Community Church. He said in his sermon on Sunday, January 15, 2017,

> I remember early on in my life as a parent, I remember getting on my knees and asking God to forgive me for messed up priorities. I made a commitment to Him that with all my heart, like in everything else, I was going to be a father … I wrote down what my priorities should be as a Christian father.
>
> Priority #1
> I am a Person and I have a relationship with God.
>
> Priority #2
> I am a Partner and I have a relationship with my spouse.
>
> Priority #3
> I am a Parent and I have a relationship with my children.
>
> Priority #4
> Then I am a Pastor and I have a relationship with my church. (Jeremiah, 2017)

I respectfully pray and ask that all clergy teach the foundational scriptures of family that were not included in *The Purpose Driven Life*, such as Ephesians 5:25 as previously quoted. Another scripture that was not include in that book but should be *first* in our lives is 1 Timothy 5:4 (NIV): "First of all to put their religion into practice by caring for their own family," and verse 8, "Anyone who does not provide for their relatives, and especially for their own household, has denied the faith and is worse than an unbeliever."

God says our family should come first before the church. If pastors have young children, then the evidence revealing if they qualify to pastor should be based on how they raise their children. The Bible says an overseer, pastor, or bishop must be "one who rules his own house well, having his children in submission with all reverence (for if a man does not know how to rule his own house, how will he take care of the church of God?") (1 Timothy 3:4–5 NKJV).

I believe God has commissioned me to write this book in order to correct the error in his book and in traditional teaching and let Christians know that our first ministry is our spouse and children.

God led me to read *The Purpose Driven Life* in 2013 even though I had already read it in 2003. This time, God revealed to me the alteration of scripture and how God's principle in Ephesians 5:25 was changed. He also showed me how we open ourselves and our family up to the enemy when we don't follow His Word. God tells us what is right in order to protect us, not to control us.

I want to be very careful and sensitive to how I deliver this message. My motive is to help leaders and the whole body of Christ protect their families and prevent tragedy.

On April 6, 2013, Pastor Rick Warren's son committed suicide. I believe Pastor Warren to be a genuine man of God. I received many great teachings from his book. I prayed daily for him and his family and at the same time sought God to understand how this could happen. Pastor Gary Keesee of Faith Life Church near Columbus, Ohio, teaches Christians to be "spiritual scientists" and to find out why something went wrong when something does, just like the disciples did in Mark 9:28. All of Pastor Keesee's five children have lived for God from childhood to adulthood.

As a spiritual scientist and a follower of Pastor Keesee's teaching, I needed to know why Pastor Warren's son committed suicide in order to help possibly prevent the tragedy of suicide in my family and anyone else's. Since suicide is a leading cause of death in America, everyone needs to know how to prevent this type of tragedy in his or her family. I was in the middle of reading Purpose #2, "You were formed for God's family," where Pastor Rick Warren teaches, "Your spiritual family is even more important than your physical family because it will last forever" (Warren, 2002). God showed me that when we put our spiritual family (the church) before our physical family, we open the door for the enemy to attack our family with drugs, lust, suicide, toxic relationships, and anything else the devil can use to destroy us. It is not God's will for us to live in tragedy. I'm not saying someone cannot go to heaven after committing suicide; that is between that person and God. I'm saying that suicide and tragedy are not God's will for us, God does not cause it, and we can prevent it in our children if we prioritize our family God's way and teach others to do the same.

Jesus said, "The thief does not come except to steal, and to kill, and to destroy. I have come that they may have life, and that they may have it more abundantly" (John 10:10 NKJV).

Jesus put the church family first because it was his wife and children. He was married to the church, and therefore, He put the church family before His mother and brothers (Mark 3:31–35). Jesus quotes Genesis 2:24 when He says, "'For this reason a man shall leave his father and mother and be joined to his wife, and the two shall become one flesh.'

So then, they are no longer two but one flesh. Therefore what God has joined together, let not man separate" (Matthew 19:5–6 NKJV).

What God wants us to do is prioritize our own families before the church family. In your effort to love your children, make sure they feel loved. We must esteem and love our children properly to make sure they fulfill God's will for their lives from birth to burial.

Chapter 14

This Way They Won't Depart

Train up a child in the way he should go, and
when he is old he will not depart from it.
—Proverbs 22:6 (NKJV)

Probability or promise?

Some believe that the Proverbs were never intended to be absolute promises from God. They believe they are probabilities of things that are likely to occur. I do agree that many Proverbs are probabilities and not promises from God, such as Proverbs 10:4: "Lazy hands make a man poor, but diligent hands bring wealth." We all may have met a diligently working Christian who is poor. I know I have. However, I firmly believe that some of the Proverbs are promises from God, such as Proverbs 21:21 (NKJV): "He who follows righteousness and mercy finds life, righteousness, and honor." I do not believe that if you follow righteousness and mercy you may probably find life (speaking of life everlasting). That would suggest that if you follow righteousness and mercy, there is a possibility you may find death and hell. Another promise in Proverbs is 22:9 (NKJV): "He who has a generous eye will be blessed, For he gives of his bread to the poor." God promises you will be blessed as a result of your giving. Finally, Proverbs 22:6 is another promise from God that lines up with the rest of God's Word: "Train up a child in the way he should go, and when he is old he will not depart from it." It means exactly what it says. If you train children in the way they should go, then when they are old, they will not depart from it. I believe it is a promise.

If someone does not believe it is a promise, there can be some negative results that follow. Many people have seen children turn out to be such horrible adults that they don't want to have children. They don't want to have children because they have been deceived into thinking that even a Christian parent can train a child right and the child can still be a horrible adult.

Another negative result of parents not believing this verse is a promise is the low expectation of their children. The expectation parents have for their children has a lot to do with the expectation their children have for themselves. When society is trying so hard to warp the minds of our children, we need to stand on the Word of God. Because there are Christian parents who do not believe their children can live according to God's promises, many don't expect them to live for God throughout their lives. Several parents told me that all our children will need to be prodigals and live in sin for a period of time. The devil is a liar, and this is one of his lies!

Instead of stressing the importance of abstinence, they stress the importance of "safe sex" with a condom. The thinking is *Why even teach abstinence when they are going to do it anyway?*

The body of Christ needs to know that we can train our children in a way that will result in our children being what God wants them to be. And we can make sure our children live lives fully committed to the Lord and do not go to the lake of fire. That is not God's will. God's will is clear. In 2 Peter 3:9 (NIV), it says, "The Lord is not slow in keeping his promise, as some understand slowness. He is patient with you, not wanting anyone to perish, but everyone to come to repentance."

Does that mean that if a child goes to hell or lives in sin, it is all the parents' fault? *No.* First of all, the parents cannot be blamed because then the parents could just blame their parents. In addition, you cannot put the blame on the grandparents because they may have done better than the great-grandparents. If you can blame the great-grandparents, then it eventually becomes all Adam and Eve's fault, and even they blamed someone else.

The second reason the child's lifestyle is not all the parents' fault is the parents could be alcoholics, child abusers, or drug users, yet they could still have a child who chooses to live a life fully committed to the Lord Jesus Christ in spite of the terrible example and experience of his or her parents. Therefore, it is the decision of each individual to respond to the gospel accordingly.

Finally, the child's lifestyle is not the parents' fault because the Bible says it's not the parents fault. Ezekiel 18:20 (NIV) says, "The one who sins is the one who will die. The child will not share the guilt of the parent, nor will the parent share the guilt of the child. The righteousness of the righteous will be credited to them, and the wickedness of the wicked will be charged against them." The whole eighteenth chapter of Ezekiel really makes it plain that the parents are not ultimately responsible for whether the child goes to heaven or hell.

I am saying that God promises there are things parents can do to make certain their children do not live in sin and will ultimately enter the kingdom of heaven. But let's look at some arguments against that.

One argument is that Adam and Eve were handled with perfection by God Himself in a perfect environment, yet they still stumbled into sin. However, Proverbs 22:6 would not apply to Adam and Eve simply because they were never children. The scripture says, "Train up a child," and he or she won't depart, not train up an adult. In contrast, God did have a son who was trained as a child and did not even sin at all. His name was Jesus, and he was the last Adam (1 Corinthians 15:45).

I would like to make sure I am not misunderstood so I will make this statement with certainty: *your children will sin*. There is no way to prevent your children from ever sinning. "For all have sinned and fall short of the glory of God" (Romans 3:23 NKJV). However, you can prevent your children from living in sin. There is a huge difference. Romans 6:1–2 (NIV) says, "Shall we go on sinning so that grace may increase? By no means! We died to sin; how can we live in it any longer?" There is also 1 John 3:9 (NIV): "No one who is born of God will continue to sin, because God's seed remains in him; he cannot go on sinning, because he has been born of God."

Let's look at some other points that may suggest parents cannot guarantee their children will commit and stay committed to the Lord. Cain's parents were not blamed for his murder, Jacob was not blamed for the differences between Joseph's righteousness and his brother's wickedness, and Samuel was not charged with the rebellious sin of his children. On the surface, these seem to be valid points, yet the Bible does indirectly tell us these parents could have prevented their children's rebellion but they did not follow the eight principles in this book.

Most of us are well aware of the sin of Adam and Eve; therefore, we know they did not practice holiness. As I mentioned in chapter 8, Jacob did not love his children's mother properly. He did not love his children properly either. He made a special coat for only one child, which, of course, provoked the other children to wrath. Samuel had his future declared, and he was committed to the Lord, but unfortunately, he did not do the same thing for his children. When parents follow these principles, the end result is always a child who is pleasing to God.

Another definition of train is "a line or succession of persons or things following one after the other" (*Merriam-Webster*, 2016).

I've had the opportunity to visit many churches, and I noticed that even when children do come to church, parents too often miss the opportunity to train them, train them as in have their children follow them in doing God's work like a caboose on a train. As soon as they get to church, the parents go one way and the children go another. Now, if your children are going to be with someone who is training them in praise and worship and such things, that is great. The problem occurs when many of our parents are praising in the front of the church, while their children are playing in the back of the church.

I've seen children playing, talking, passing notes, texting, and using their electronics during service while remaining oblivious to the speaker. If we do not train them to take the things of God seriously, most of them will not do it on their own. Please do not let your children sit in the back, disengaged from the service. If you are active during church and cannot be with your children, then sit them next to someone you want them to imitate.

Even during choir rehearsal or other times we are at the church, we can include our children in the opening and closing prayer. You can keep your eyes open to watch them. Train them to close their eyes so they are not playing and can focus on God. The Bible tells us to "watch and pray" (Matthew 26:41 NKJV). Watch, and make sure your children are connected next to you when you are doing works for God.

Many people have misinterpreted Proverbs 22:6 to say something it does not say. I have been in church for over three decades and cannot count how many times I have heard this scripture applied as a promise that those who have fallen away from Christ will come back. The scripture does not say, "Train up a child in the way he should go, and when he departs from it, he will return when he is old." It says, "He will not depart," as in, he will never depart. Yet, if your children have departed, there are still scriptures you can stand on for them to return to a committed relationship to Christ.

If your teenage or adult children are living in sin, I believe if you have planted godly seeds in them, by bringing them to church and teaching them the Word of God, they have a great chance of returning to Christ! I believe this because of this scripture: Galatians 6:7 (NIV), "Do not be deceived: God cannot be mocked. A man reaps what he sows." If you have sown godly seeds, believe God they will come to fruition. Prayer can always make a big difference in whether someone comes back to Christ or not. "Pray for one another, that you may be healed. The effective, fervent prayer of a righteous man avails much" (James 5:16b NKJV).

For a more in-depth look at this scripture, we will go to the amplified version.

Proverbs 22:6 in the Amplified Bible (AMP) says, "Train up a child in the way he should go [and in keeping with his individual gift or bent], and when he is old he will not depart from it."

Each child has individual abilities God has given him or her to fulfill His purpose. You can't make your child be a professional singer or football or baseball player unless he or she has the God-given potential to do so. In the same way, you can't make him or her be a doctor, lawyer, or preacher, unless he or she has the God-given potential within. A lot of people are telling their children, "You can be anything you want to be," but that is not exactly accurate. You can't be anything you want to be, but you can be anything God wants you to be. Some people want to be a singer, and they think they sound like Mariah Carey, but they really sound more like Jim Carrey. *Find your individual gift.*

No matter what career path they pursue, God wants you to know you can train your children in such a way that they will never leave Christ even when they leave your house.

Chapter 15

The Bill Cosby Complex

For what profit is it to a man if he gains the
whole world, and loses his own soul?
-Matthew 16:26a (NKJV).

As I was growing up, Bill Cosby was my role model. He seemed to have achieved success in every important area of life. In the area of family, he was known as "America's favorite dad"; in education, he had earned a doctorate; and as far as status, career, and fame, he was second to none in the United States. Financially, he was a billionaire, and he did more good with his money than most. You could not have much more success than that, could you?

The problem was he was unsuccessful spiritually. He was living in sin and was not faithful to his wife. I don't know if he did everything some have accused him of, but being unfaithful is enough. Regardless of the good you do and the success you accomplish, if you fail spiritually, your sin can negate all your other accomplishments.

When parents focus on education, position, and financial success more than salvation, they create what I call the Bill Cosby complex.

"For what profit is it to a man if he gains the whole world, and loses his own soul?" (Matthew 16:26a NKJV).

Test yourself. If you don't require your children to pray or receive God's Word daily, but you do require them to do their homework, sport, or extracurricular activity daily, you have actually been training them to put these things before God's priorities. You've created the Bill Cosby complex.

Education minus salvation still equals damnation, but education plus salvation equals a perfect combination.

In this day and age, I believe the only way to guarantee our children's salvation is to start them off in homeschool or Christian school in elementary. If you put your kids in a public school in today's society, you will have to fight all the bad seeds they will sow into your child on a daily basis.

The School System

In the early 1800s, many were illiterate in America. However, people taught their children to read so they could read the Bible. That was one of the purposes of school. Look how far we have come from that today. The schools continued to be run mostly by Christian churches until the 1890s, at which point states started to take control of the existing schools. As a part of the daily curriculum, students were taught to pray and read, using the Bible. As the twentieth century began, many classrooms started each day with the pledge of allegiance, a prayer, and a reading from the Bible ("School Prayer in America," 2013).

In 1962, the Supreme Court determined in the case of *Engle v. Vitale* that it was unconstitutional for state officials to require the recitation of an official school prayer in public schools (uscourts.gov, 2016). Then the Supreme Court declared on June 17, 1963, that school-sponsored Bible reading in public schools was also unconstitutional, during the case of *Abington Township School District v. Schempp* (*District of Abington Township v. Schempp*, 2014).

Taking out the spiritual teaching in school actually hurt our nation educationally as well as morally. Since prayer and Bible reading were taken out of schools, SAT scores declined rapidly for eighteen consecutive years; the rapid decline slowed down amid the explosion of private religious schools. The United States had one thousand private religious schools in 1965 and then thirty-two thousand in the period 1974 to 1984 ("What Happened When Prayer Was Taken out of Schools," 2009). Students can still pray and read their Bibles at school on their own time, but prayer and the Bible can't be imposed by a school official.

The court may have taken corporate prayer and Bible reading out of the schools, but it is our fault we left it out of the home. And we will not ultimately be judged by the Supreme Court, but we will be judged by the Supreme God. We must repent and bring daily prayer and Bible reading back into our homes or our own families and communities will continue to decline.

Tragic deaths have increased in our schools and society not just because of what our courts took out but because of what they allow in. From preschool to postgraduate, the teaching of macroevolution from a single organism attacks the value of every life. On November 12, 1968, the United States Supreme Court case *Epperson v. Arkansas* started the trend of evolution being taught in the schools (Robinson, 2016). Some jurisdictions tried to require the teaching of both evolution and creation science, but in 1987, in the case of *Edwards v. Aguillard*, the Supreme Court ruled that unconstitutional (*Edwards v. Aguilard*, 2014).

When children are taught there is no God, they believe they can kill other children and then kill themselves with no other consequences. They think they are their own justice system. They will realize how wrong they were when they wake up to God's judgment after death. "And as it is appointed for men to die once, but after this the judgment" (Hebrews 9:27 NKJV).

This is the same terrifying thinking that causes people to justify revenge, students against teachers and other students, men against police and other men. They don't understand that justice will come either in this life or the next. "Do not take revenge, my dear friends, but leave room for God's wrath, for it is written: 'It is mine to avenge; I will repay,' says the Lord" (Romans 12:19 NIV).

"If there was no God, we would all be 'accidents,' the result of astronomical random chance in the universe. Life would have no purpose or meaning or significance. There would be no right or wrong, and no hope beyond your brief years here on earth" (Warren, 2002).

The public schools preach tolerance, but they practice more and more intolerance of everything that is Christian. Instead of being neutral, they have become anti-God. They are teaching a theory as fact, even though it cannot be scientifically proven and actually goes against true science. The changing of species cannot be scientifically proven because that would take millions of years to prove. "No one has ever demonstrated one species changing to another species," says neurologist Dr. Ben Carson (Chapman, 2015).

Dr. Carson was the head of pediatric neurosurgery at Johns Hopkins. Ben Carson, MD, was considered the greatest pediatric neurosurgeon in the world, and in 2016, the retired neurosurgeon was a presidential candidate. This neurologist was the first person to successfully separate conjoined twins at the head and invented the procedure to do so (McLennan Distinguished Lecture Series, 2011). Dr. Carson adds, "I do believe God created us. In fact, the more you know about God, and the deeper your relationship with God, I think the more intricate becomes your knowledge of the way things work, including the human body" (Carson, 2011).

It is a scientific fact that every seed reproduces after its own kind (species). Science agrees with the Bible. "Then God said, 'Let the earth bring forth living creatures according to (limited to, consistent with) their kind: livestock, crawling things, and wild animals of the earth according to their kinds'; and it was so [because He had spoken them into creation]" (Genesis 1:24 AMP). Dr. Carson has proven that acknowledging God can help us in the science and medical fields. Yet, secular liberals have forced the schools to teach this macroevolution to avoid acknowledging God as our creator.

Most of us are not neurologists; therefore, we have to choose what we believe based off of what others tell us. It seems to take more blind faith to believe that humans have come from fish on accident, then it does to believe in a God who has created us on purpose. One science journalist said, "You can see a transition between a fish and a land creature in fossils and genes only if you have a vivid imagination" (Darwin Fish Lacks Tetrapod Legs, 2016).

The public schools and our American society have become so anti-Christ that they have taken (and are continuing to take) BC and AD from our history books. *BC* stands for "Before Christ," and *AD* stands for the Latin term *Anno Domini*, which means "the year of our Lord." They are replacing BC with BCE, "before the common era," and replacing AD with CE, "common era." I believe our children should know BCE and CE (just as they should know about the theory of evolution). However, I don't believe that in the United States, BCE and CE should replace BC and AD as our common terms. Again, they say we need to be tolerant, but they cannot even tolerate the terms BC and AD (even though Jesus was technically born about 4 BC).

Jesus says He sends out sheep among wolves, not lambs. In other words, kids are lambs in elementary school and their belief in God is preyed upon by the wolves against God. Even though there are Christian clubs in secular schools and students can read their Bible and pray on their own in public schools, according to the First Amendment (Haynes, 2011), they are still lambs among wolves in the secular public schools at the elementary level.

Jesus said, "Behold, I send you out as sheep in the midst of wolves. Therefore be wise as serpents and harmless as doves" (Matthew 10:16 NKJV).

Homeschooling or private school educations are even found to get the best results in middle school and high school. "The home-educated typically score 15 to 30 percentile points above public-school students on standardized academic achievement tests. A 2015 study found Black homeschool students to be scoring 23 to 42 percentile points above Black public school students" (Ray, 2016). "Private school students generally perform higher than their public school counterparts on standardized achievement tests" (Chen, 2015).

We should want our children to get a good education. We should demand it. We need to make sure they are doing their homework. If they are not or they are struggling in school, we need to find out why. Don't miss the parent-teacher conferences. Be sure to meet with the teachers. I believe those things are necessary. The problem is schools have philosophies that attack God and God's Word. They are trying to brain wash your child into thinking God does not exist. Therefore, our children will miss their purpose in life. Jesus said to love God and love your neighbor as yourself sums up the true meaning of life and the whole Bible (Matthew 22:37–39).

If we are saying that our children don't have time to pray and read the Bible every day and can never make it to Bible class because of homework, athletics, and extracurricular activities, we are training our kids to put God last instead of first.

"But first and most importantly seek (aim at, strive after) His kingdom and His righteousness [His way of doing and being right—the attitude and character of God], and all these things will be given to you also" (Matthew 6:33 AMP).

Chapter 16

How to Prevent Same-Sex Attractions

Love never fails.
-1 Corinthians 13:8a (NKJV)

F irst, let's look at some definitions to better identify exactly what we are talking about.

Sexual orientation is one's natural preference in sexual partners, a predilection for homosexuality, heterosexuality, or bisexuality (dictionary.com, Sexual Orientation, 2016). Even though homosexuality is a very common word, many people do not know there are two very different definitions. According dictionary.com, homosexuality can be defined in two ways:

1. Sexual orientation to persons of the same sex.
2. Sexual activity with another of the same sex.

According to God's law, only one of these definitions is a sin. Having a homosexual orientation is simply a desire for the same sex. Just being attracted to the same sex is not a sin.

> When tempted, no one should say, 'God is tempting me.' For God cannot be tempted by evil, nor does he tempt anyone; but each person is tempted when they

are dragged away by their own evil desire and enticed. Then, after desire has conceived, it gives birth to sin; and sin, when it is full-grown, gives birth to death. (James 1:13–15 NIV).

We see here that desire itself is not sin, but if it is not aborted, it will give birth to sin. Again the Bible says, "So I say, walk by the Spirit, and you will not gratify the desires of the flesh. For the flesh desires what is contrary to the Spirit, and the Spirit what is contrary to the flesh. They are in conflict with each other, so that you are not to do whatever you want" (Galatians 5:16–17 NIV). Desiring or wanting to do something sinful does not necessarily make it a sin as long as given the opportunity you do not (or would not) gratify or fulfill that desire.

The second definition of homosexuality is a sin. This involves sexual activity or sexual contact. "Do you not know that wrongdoers will not inherit the kingdom of God? Do not be deceived: Neither the sexually immoral, nor idolaters, nor adulterers, nor men who have sex with men, nor thieves, nor the greedy, nor drunkards, nor slanderers, nor swindlers will inherit the kingdom of God" (1 Corinthians 6:9–10 NIV). This is very clear that men having sex with men is sin (some versions may say homosexuals, but the correct interpretation in our time is men having sex with other men or homosexual offenders).

Another reference where God condemns homosexual acts is in the first chapter of Romans:

Therefore God gave them over in the sinful desires of their hearts to sexual impurity for the degrading of their bodies with one another. They exchanged the truth about God for a lie, and worshiped and served created things rather than the Creator—who is forever praised. Amen. Because of this, God gave them over to shameful lusts. Even their women exchanged natural sexual relations for unnatural ones. In the same way, the men also abandoned natural relations with women and were inflamed with lust for one another. Men committed shameful acts with other men, and received in themselves the due penalty for their error. (Romans 1:24–27 NIV).

I also deem it necessary to define the word *gay*. Gay is pertaining to or exhibiting sexual desire or behavior directed toward a person or persons of one's own sex (dictionary.com, 2016). In this definition, they put desire and behavior into the same definition, which is why it is important to find out what people mean (especially if the person is a child) when they identify themselves as gay. Are they participating in gay activity, or do they simply have same-sex desires?

According to the sixth edition of the *Publication Manual of the American Psychological Association*, "For a person having a bisexual orientation, the orientation is not chosen even though the sex of the partner may be a choice" (2010). According to the book, *gay* can be interpreted broadly to include men and women but most often to include only men.

From my years of research through books, doctors, acquaintances, close friends, and family who claim to be gay, ex-gay, lesbian, bisexual, transgender, queer, questioning, or curious and the like, I agree that most people who have same-sex desires did not choose to have them. The desire was not a choice but came on its own because of multiple possible factors. At the same time, having sexual contact with the same sex is a choice. This is also why the desire is not a sin, yet choosing to fulfill the desire is a sin.

Previously many thought the questions of sexual orientation could be solved scientifically. The theory was that there was a gay gene and the cause was probably genetic. However, this is not the issue; it really does not matter what desires someone is born with. Some may be born with the desire for multiple sex partners, some may be born with the desire to get drunk, and some even suggest they were born with the desire to have sex with children. All these desires must be properly dealt with, and it is a sin to choose to fulfill them. In 1973, the APA voted and determined that homosexuality was no longer a psychiatric disorder. Now some of those who advocated for that change are trying to remove an adult's desire to have sex with a child as a disorder as well.

Even if a man says he is attracted to other men, if he chooses to commit to one man, then he still has to deny himself from pursuing the other men he is attracted to. Therefore, he cannot pursue all desires. Denying ourselves is something we all must do. To be spiritually healthy, we must deny sinful desires, just as if we want to be physically healthy we must deny ourselves the unhealthy foods we desire.

Then Jesus said to His disciples, "Whoever wants to be my disciple must deny themselves and take up their cross and follow me" (Matthew 16:24 NIV).

Now let us look at a story from the Bible that reveals how children can be born different. Some girls will enjoy things traditionally associated with boys, and some boys will enjoy things traditionally associated with girls, but this does not mean they will desire or should pursue a desire to be intimate with the same sex. These points stood out in my spirit as I read it one day. Men and women are born different from birth; this does not mean they are born gay. Furthermore, we should not try to label them as gay simply because they prefer not to do things our society traditionally associates with their gender.

> And the Lord said to her: "Two nations are in your womb, two peoples shall be separated from your body; one people shall be stronger than the other, and the older shall serve the younger."
> So when her days were fulfilled for her to give birth, indeed there were twins in her womb. And the first came out red. He was like a hairy garment all over; so they called his name Esau (hairy). Afterward his brother

came out, and his hand took hold of Esau's heel; so his name was called Jacob. Isaac was sixty years old when she bore them. So the boys grew. And Esau was a skillful hunter, a man of the field; but Jacob was a mild man, dwelling in tents. And Isaac loved Esau because he ate of his game (hunted animals), but Rebekah loved Jacob.

Now Jacob cooked a stew; and Esau came in from the field, and he was weary. And Esau said to Jacob, "Please feed me with that same red stew, for I am weary" (Genesis 25:23–30 NKJV).

Both of these are men. Yet, God created them differently and gifted them differently. Esau was a skilled hunter. In today's time, Esau would have been considered a jock or a good athlete. This kind of boy typically enjoys wrestling, football, basketball, boxing, baseball, outdoor sports, or another sport our Western society associates with masculinity. Jacob was a mild man. In today's time, he might be considered sensitive or artistic, maybe the kind of boy who enjoys cooking, drawing, dancing, acting, singing, or something to that effect, and they are generally not into traditionally male sports. Many of these boys God has gifted in music. There are many boys who are strong on both sides, such as King David, who loved music and dancing and played the harp but was also a great warrior in battle.

We cannot put boys in a box, as if they must be either mild or macho. The point is boys and girls are born different. Whether we consider a boy born mild or macho, either one could develop same-sex attractions. Some boys are milder and seem to be in the minority, while others are born more macho, as we call it. They play rougher and seem to be in the majority.

According to Dr. Joseph Nicolosi, an expert in homosexuality, when the boys who are born milder don't make the proper connection with their parents, specifically their fathers or their male peers, they often develop same-sex attractions (Nicolosi and Nicolosi, 2003). Also a girl who does not connect with her mother emotionally can develop same-sex attractions.

Joe Dallas is the coauthor of *The Complete Christian Guide to Understanding Homosexuality* (Dallas and Heche, 2010). He lectures and heads a biblical counseling practice in California. Dallas himself was a former practicing gay man who has successfully left the lifestyle for Christ since 1984. He also wrote, *Desires in Conflict: Hope for Men Who Struggle with Sexual Identity*, republished in 2003 (Dallas, 2003). This book has helped shape my personal views, and much of this report is influenced by his books. I recommend his books if you have a child or anyone close to you who is seriously struggling with same-sex attractions.

In his book, Dallas describes that even though there is no biological evidence that a person can be born gay, it has been shown that there may be biological influences that could predispose a person toward same-sex desires. The important word here is *predispose*, as in "having a tendency toward something"(Dallas, 2003). Individuals can be born with predispositions toward any number of problems—alcoholism and depression are two examples. This doesn't make the problems inevitable. It is the environment or nurturing that brings predispositions to be fulfilled.

How does a child develop sexual desires for the same sex?

Dallas believes homosexual attractions develop in a child along these lines:

1. A child's perception of his or her relationship to parents or significant others.
2. A child's emotional response to those perceptions.
3. Emotional needs arising from these perceptions and responses.
4. The sexualization of those emotional needs. (Dallas, 2003).

This allows for many different childhood experiences, placing the emphasis not so much on what did or didn't happen but on the way the child perceived it. That helps us understand the variety of childhood histories found in homosexually oriented adults. Some actually had excellent parents, while some were raised by horrible parents. It was often their perception of their early relationships, not necessarily the reality, that generated a response.

Here is a general example. A boy is raised by a father who loves him, spends time with him, and provides well for all his family. Then through circumstances outside of the father's control, he has to take on a second job, which forces him away from the home. The boy is too young to understand the financial situation. All he knows is that Dad is not around, and he takes that as a personal rejection. It does not matter whether his father has actually rejected him. He perceives his father's absence as rejection and responds as a result of that feeling. He feels hurt, develops bitterness toward his father, and emotionally withdraws from the person he feels rejected by.

In another family, a boy is raised by a father who blatantly rejects him. He makes it obvious by telling his son that he wishes he had never been born and that he wants nothing to do with him. This child too feels hurt, develops bitterness toward his father, and emotionally withdraws from the person he feels rejected by. Two children from completely different parents responded to early pain in the same way. Both have experienced disconnect in their relationship with the parent of the same sex, and both have responded emotionally to that disconnect.

A perception creates an emotional response, and an emotional response creates emotional needs. Emotional needs in many cases can and do become sexualized. As a result, they have sexual attractions toward the same gender that they have emotional needs toward. The sexual attractions then turn into sexual desires.

We mentioned *The Five Love Languages* before. One of them is physical touch. Our children desire the loving touch of both male and female, mother and father. If they do not receive the love through a nurturing hug and kiss from a loving female and a loving male, it may turn into a sexual desire during puberty. A female who does not get that loving touch from a father regularly may become promiscuous with other men. In the same way, a boy who does not get that loving touch from his father may become promiscuous with other men also. It depends on the child's makeup and love language.

We should understand that these are simply two examples, and that homosexuality is very complex. We can say that homosexual acts in all forms are immoral and goes against God's intended design. However, most generalizations we make on the matter will not be sufficient. There is not really a typical homosexual. There is not simply one reason people become homosexual. And there is not simply one method of dealing with homosexuality that will be effective for every man or woman. An intellectual and respectful discussion of same-sex attractions and actions should include a respect for its diversity.

"Greet one another with a holy kiss. The churches of Christ greet you" (Romans 16:16 NKJV). At least four times, the Bible says to greet one another with a "holy kiss." Some things cannot be healed by simply reading the Bible but only by doing what it says. Some men need love shown with a pure embrace and kiss on the cheek, things they may not have received regularly from their dads.

A long time ago, my wife and I were praying for a man at the altar, and my wife whispered to me, "God says you need to put your hand on his back."

I whispered back, "I'm not about to put my hand on another man's back."

She said it again. I felt that even though I was uncomfortable, I needed to do it. As I put my hand on his back, he began to cry a little, and I felt emotional healing taking place.

Then she said, "God says to rub your hand across his back."

I responded, "I'm not about to rub my hand across another man's back." I realized that God had to talk to her because if He just told me, I would rebuke that thought, fearing it might be the devil trying to make me gay. The devil is a liar! However, as I was obedient to the Holy Spirit and rubbed his back, the man began to weep, and God was able to do a greater emotional healing in him. At the same time God was healing him, he was healing me of my insecurities and fear (homophobia). The Bible says, "There is no fear in love; but perfect love casts out fear, because fear involves torment. But he who fears has not been made perfect in love" (1 John 4:18 NKJV).

A currently increasing problem in our society is many people labeling the boys who are born milder and girls who seem to be macho as gay before they have a chance to decide what kind of relationship they want to be in. So how does a boy develop more feminine mannerisms than masculine mannerisms?

The answer is often quite simple. It is most commonly because he is simply around more females. It's called Imprinting. This imprinting is talked about in the book *The Nature and Nurture of Love: From Imprinting to Attachment in Cold War America Publisher* (Vicedo, 2013). Imprinting is rapid learning that occurs during a brief receptive period, typically soon after birth, and establishes along- lasting behavioral response to a specific individual, individuals, or parent (dictionary.com, 2016).

Children will generally behave like those they are around. They will pick up their voice tones, hand gestures, mannerisms, even walk like them many times without any effort. When you see a boy acting feminine, do not be prejudice and prejudge him to be gay. He most likely has what you perceive as feminine mannerisms because he has been around females the majority of the time, most often his mother. This is why many children that grow up with a parent that has an accent will pick up that same accent. Do you know someone who was born in the United States, but speaks with an accent of their parent from another country? That is an example of imprinting.

Whether it is a male with feminine mannerisms or a girl with masculine mannerisms, they should not be condemned, ridiculed, or ostracized. Even though it is likely they will be tested with same sex attractions, we should not assume they are practicing homosexual behavior. We all are tested with many things, and God would rather have a person who has same sex attractions practice abstinence, than a person with heterosexual attractions being promiscuous. "For this is the will of God, your sanctification: that you should abstain from sexual immorality" (1Thessalonians 4:3 NKJV).

According to Dr. Joseph Nicolosi, our children need "the three A's"— affirmation, attention, and affection—from both a mother and a father figure, especially a father they see as strong and benevolent, in order to prevent same-sex attractions. If children are abused sexually, verbally, mentally, or physically by a parent or someone else, it can result in emotional problems, and they can develop strong attractions to the same sex.

There are many different levels of same-sex attractions. Here is a scale listing sexual attractions, which helps us understand that it is not just about being gay, bisexual, or straight, and one does not simply change from gay to straight or from straight to gay. Change takes place in degrees. This Kinsey scale was first discovered by Dr. Alfred Kinsey, an author of *Sexual Behavior in the Human Male* (Kinsey, 1948).

0   Exclusively heterosexual, no homosexual attractions
1. Predominantly heterosexual, incidental homosexual attractions
2. Predominantly heterosexual, more than incidental homosexual attractions
3. Equally heterosexual and homosexual attractions
4. Predominantly homosexual, more than incidental heterosexual attractions
5. Predominantly homosexual, incidental heterosexual attractions
6. Exclusively homosexual attractions

Joe Dallas describes that homosexuality exists to degrees, and an individual is able to change by degrees. So a person who rates a Kinsey 6 is not likely to jump right to a point 1 or 0 (not to deny the possibility).

If our children are not abused and receive regular affirmation, affection, and attention from a mother and father figure they view as benevolent (good and loving), they will not develop same-sex attractions above a level 3 on the Kinsey scale. If their mother or father is not available for whatever reason, children will need a mother and a father figure that they respect to provide these things regularly.

In many cases where a good father (or mother) is not around, you will need to find a father figure who can spend two hours of quality time a week (or at least every two weeks) with the child doing something the child enjoys (such as a sport or a variety of other activities), but not just watching a movie or TV because then what they are watching has the father's attention instead of the child.

I spent time with my godson, who did not have his father in his life. I wanted to exercise with him to help him to get healthier, but he did not like basketball, football, or other exercise activities I liked. After some research effort with trial and error, we found out he liked *Dance Dance Revolution*, a video game that you dance to on the Wii; therefore, we enjoyed playing that together. He was really good at it. As a result, I was able to provide him with affirmation, attention, and affection. He got healthier, he felt loved, and even though he dominated me in the game, we both had a great time together.

We all need love from both a male and a female. It takes both to conceive a child, and it takes both for the child to be emotionally healthy. If a child does not have them, it does not mean he or she will definitely develop same-sex attractions, but he or she will develop a problem in one area or another as a result of what he or she is missing. It could result in anger issues or a number of things. Every child needs to feel loved by both a mother figure and a father figure.

Remember that the issue of homosexuality is very complex and not one situation fits all. Even experiencing sexual abuse as a child does not always result in same-sex attractions (SSAs). SSAs are only one of many problems that can come from sexual abuse or parents who are not emotionally healthy themselves. Yet, with God's help and guidance, we can apply these principles and prevent our children from struggling with same-sex attractions.

Chapter 17

Thanking for the Spanking

Do not withhold discipline from the child; If you swat him
with a reed-like rod [applied with godly wisdom], he will not
die. You shall swat him with the reed-like rod And rescue his
life from Sheol (the netherworld, the place of the dead).
—Proverbs 23:13–14 (AMP)

W hen I was a little boy growing up, I loved my childhood.
My mother went out of her way to spend quality time with
us, taking us to play and picking up family and friends.
Mom would show us love and create a happy, healthy, and fun but safe
environment. She made me feel loved and protected. She only spanked
me when it was necessary. Mom was consistent with love, which included
rewards and discipline. She truly earned the trust of my brother and me
and even our extended family. I am so thankful for my mother's training.

I have never told her off. I have never yelled at her or even thought about
raising my hand at her, even when I was obviously bigger and stronger
than she was. I would like to take the time to thank my mother and
father for appropriately spanking me. That's right; I'm thanking them
for the spanking.

I was never suspended for fighting. I avoided fights like a plague. I was
less concerned about facing a peer and more concerned about facing
my mom.

We should truly judge corrective discipline by the fruit or long-term results. In the short term and long term, spanking benefitted me tremendously. Matthew 7:19–20 (AMP) says, "Every tree that does not bear good fruit is cut down and cast into the fire. Therefore, you will fully know them by their fruits." The fruit of spanking God's way is a child you take delight in.

The Bible is clear on the importance of spanking our children when it is necessary. Please do not avoid this form of discipline. There is a saying that goes, "Spare the rod; spoil the child." Although this is not a scripture in the Bible, the Bible clearly agrees with the concept.

How can we be sure that spanking is God's way? Let's look into the scriptures. Proverbs has the most information about this subject of disciplining your child. Even Hebrews 12:5–6, a New Testament scripture, quoted Proverbs 3:11 and 12 when the Bible spoke of a father's discipline. Because Hebrews quotes Proverbs to understand God's discipline, we know how applicable the Proverbs are for the New Testament saints, especially when it comes to disciplining our children.

Proverbs 3:5–6 (NKJV) says, "Trust in the LORD with all your heart, And lean not on your own understanding; In all your ways acknowledge Him, And He shall direct your paths."

This scripture is letting us know that we cannot try to use our own understanding. Many have said they have come up with a better way, such as time-out or bribes. It is true that every situation is not resolved with a spanking, and it should not be our primary method of discipline, but do not avoid the spanking when it is necessary. Don't always trust any doctor or anybody who tries to teach against God's plan. I repeat— don't lean to man's understanding when it goes against God's directing. Let God direct your path. Don't believe the lie that says when you spank your child, you will make him or her violent or you have lost control because you spank your child. Trust the Lord, not some man's so-called new understanding.

Proverbs 3:11–12 (NIV) says, "My son, do not despise the Lord's discipline and do not resent his rebuke, because the Lord disciplines those he loves, as a father the son he delights in."

One reason some pediatricians have been against spanking is because of the abuse that has taken place. Physical abuse is a serious problem and can traumatize your child. If you do not know if your child deserves a spanking for misconduct, do not spank him or her. It is better to be safe than sorry. Therefore, when in doubt, don't!

It is often tough for a parent to spank. It is easier to let a child get away with doing wrong in the short term. If we love our children, we should spank them at the proper time. This is necessary; if you don't hurt your child for a short time by spanking him or her, you will really hurt your child in the long run. If you are too tired to spank or too uncomfortable, pray that God will help you show love His way and not your own. Then you can deny your feelings of apprehension and obey God, knowing that it is better for your child in the long run.

In Dr. James Dobson's *Family Talk* (2015), he was asked when a toddler should be subjected to mild discipline. He answered, "When he openly defies his parents' spoken commands!" He said, "If he runs the other way when called, purposely slams his milk glass on the floor, dashes in the street when being told to stop, screams and throws a tantrum at bedtime, hits his friends—these are the forms of unacceptable behavior which should be discouraged. Even in these situations, however, all-out spankings are not often required to eliminate the behavior. A firm tap on the fingers or a few minutes sitting in a chair will convey the same message just as convincingly. Spankings should be reserved for a child's moments of greatest antagonism, usually occurring after the third birthday."

"He who spares his rod [of discipline] hates his son, but he who loves him disciplines diligently and punishes him early" (Proverbs 13:24 Amp).

Not only does spanking come from love; the Bible says if we spare the rod, we hate our child. Wow! I repeat—he who spares the rod hates his son. Now that is deep! The phrase "punishes him early" is very important. You will be much happier with your children if you spank them the first time they disobey you. Do not wait until you have told them several times.

Here is an example of when many parents do not spank their children early but wait until they get upset. You are on the couch, and your child grabs an ink pen he or she should not have. Then you say, "Put that down!" He or she doesn't do it. You repeat, "Put that down!" The child looks at you and thinks, *I just want to know when you will get off the couch, then I'll put this down.* The third time you get louder. "Put that down now!" The child looks at you and pauses. Then you say, "If I have to get up off this couch, I will spank your behind. You put that pen down *now!*" Again, the child doesn't move. You stand up, and the child runs to put the pen down. By this time, you are angry and frustrated. You are tempted to spank the child out of anger or severely hurt the child, all because you did not punish him or her early. To make matters worse, the child will probably repeat this pattern because he or she knows you will not do anything until you are really upset,and you don't get upset until you have to repeat yourself three or more times. That is the opposite of punishing a child early.

The verse says, "He who loves him disciplines diligently and punishes him early." Let me give you an example of punishing him early. The child picks up a pen that he or she should not have. You say, "Put that pen down!" in a normal but commanding voice. The child purposefully ignores you, and at this point, you and the child are well aware that you have been deliberately disobeyed; therefore, the child deserves a spanking. So you stand up, and then the child puts the pen down, wondering if he or she is going to be disciplined for disobeying you. You should go to the child and explain, "I said put the pen down, not put the pen down when I get up. Because you disobeyed me, you get a spanking."

I believe spanking children with a swat according to their age is appropriate. If they are two, you can use your hand and swat them on the thigh twice. When the child is four, you may get a switch or belt of some kind and spank him or her four times. The bare butt or thigh is a safe place to swat. Give the child a short time to cry, and when you know he or she should be done, let him or her go back to a normal routine.

Understanding the word *diligently* used in the verse above is very important also. You should be consistent with your discipline. Many times, it is much easier to do something once than it is to do something diligently. If you tell your child not to touch something and he deliberately touches it anyway, you should spank him. But even after you do this, your child may wonder what happens if he does it again. When your child does it again, you should spank him again. Each time your child repeats an offense, it may seem harder to discipline him for it. However, whether it is a girl or boy, we must be diligent in this manner. As a result, our children will know that we mean what we say, and they can trust our words. Our children will be more diligent in their obedience if we are diligent in our discipline.

Some have suggested that you should not spank with your hand because your hand should only be used to bless your children. However, I have found that when you use your hand to briefly spank a toddler or swat him or her on the hand, you can more easily gauge how hard you are swatting them. Also you can discipline quickly so the child can better understand the behavior that is being corrected without having to wait until you get your belt or swatting device.

In the book, *To Train Up a Child* by Michael and Debi Pearl (http://www.nogreaterjoy.org/), they state that, "In accompaniment with teaching, the properly administered spanking is restorative as nothing else can be" (Pearl, 1994). They suggest that it can remove the feeling of guilt from a child. I do agree with those particular points.

Proverbs 19:18 (AMP) says, "Discipline your son while there is hope, but do not [indulge your angry resentments by undue chastisements and] set yourself to his ruin."

The second portion of this verse says not to indulge your angry resentments by undue chastisements; this will wound your child's spirit. Never spank children out of anger. Again, many times, this is caused by delaying discipline. If your children disobey you or do something else worthy of a spanking, spank them. If you do not, then you may resent them and begin not to like them. As a result, when you spank your child, you may be in the wrong spirit and you could transfer that spirit of anger and resentment to your child. Ephesians 4:26 (NIV) says, "In your anger, do not sin: Do not let the sun go down while you are still angry." You should wait until you are not angry to spank your child. If you spank your child when you're angry, do not be surprised if your child holds anger in his or her heart as a result. Colossians 3:21 (KJV) says, "Fathers, provoke not your children to anger, lest they be discouraged."

Proverbs 22:15 (KJV) says, "Foolishness is bound up in the heart of a child, but the rod of correction will drive it far from him."

This is another scripture that emphasizes the importance of the rod and what it does. It really speaks for itself. Please do not let these scriptures fall by the wayside. Apply them.

Proverbs 29:15 (NKJV) says, "The rod and rebuke give wisdom, But a child left to himself brings shame to his mother."

If your child runs into the street and then you spank her, you have given her wisdom. It is not wise to run into the street, and now your child is wise enough to know that. Even though it may take more than one time to impart the necessary wisdom, your child will be safer as a result as well.

Proverbs 23:13–14 (Amp) says, "Withhold not discipline from the child; for if you strike and punish him with the [reedlike] rod, he will not die.

You shall whip him with the rod and deliver his life from Sheol (the place of the dead)."

This scripture really drives the point home. How can I say that the Bible guarantees your child will not go to hell without addressing spanking? Read this scripture again and understand that it is speaking to parents. "You" will deliver his soul from Sheol (hell or Hades). If you want to guarantee that your child lives a life fully committed to the Lord whether he or she is very strong-willed or not, do not completely avoid spanking. "A few small spankings when a child is very young may result in no need for any more spankings later" ("Spanking," 2016).

Some parents count down from five after giving a command before administering a spanking. My cousin used this method on her three children. She only had to briefly spank her children about twice. From then on, she never got to zero; they always quickly obeyed. The countdown even worked for the grandmother, who never even got to zero because of the precedent the mother established.

For more on this subject, I highly recommend *The New Dare to Discipline* by Dr. James Dobson (2014). If you have any questions on what to do and what not to do in disciplining your child, they will be answered with this book.

Chapter 18

Help for Single Moms

Bear one another's burdens, and so fulfill the law of Christ.
Galatians 6:2 (NKJV)

I have a special place in my heart for single moms, mainly because my brother and I were raised by one. Our mother worked hard, took care of the house, read the Bible to us, and was there on a daily basis. She worked nights in order to be there for us during the day. She helped take care of us and our grandparents who lived with us most of our childhood. My brother and I are saved today because she first introduced us to our Lord and Savior Jesus Christ. She trained us and lived a godly example in front of my brother and me, and because of this, she is my hero.

This chapter is addressed to single moms, but the information applies to single dads, coparenting and married couples, and really anyone training children as well. I was able to see firsthand the obligations of a single mom. Raising children with two parents is a tough job by itself. When we talk about a single mom, there is an overwhelming amount of work to be done. It is too much to provide for yourself and your children and then make all their meals, help with all their homework, choose all their clothes, do their laundry, nurse all their bumps and bruises, handle their emergencies, clean the house, pay the bills, transport them back and forth, fix the car, attend their events, train them, discipline them, teach them hygiene, and so on all by yourself.

Many times, mothers have no support from the child's father or anyone in the father's family. Sometimes a mom cannot get assistance from her own mother or father because of the tragedy of an early death or other circumstances, and there is no family or anyone else to help. If you do have any help, be grateful for those people, thank them, and thank God for them as well. The burden of a single parent is too much to handle alone.

"Bear one another's burdens, and so fulfill the law of Christ" (Galatians 6:2 NKJV). It's Christ's law for us to help one another and especially the single mothers. "Religion that God our Father accepts as pure and faultless is this: to look after orphans and widows in their distress and to keep oneself from being polluted by the world" (James 1:27 NIV).

This is sound advice that has helped many single mothers.

First, seek godly family members to assist with your children. Even if the person assisting is not godly, sometimes he or she can still be respectful of your beliefs and be more of a positive influence than a negative influence on your child. Pray about whom they will be around, and let the Spirit guide and provide you with people who should be in their lives.

My mom let our grandparents move in with us, which can be very hard if you want things to be done a certain way. However, if you can compromise with them, you can be a blessing to your parents and living with them could be a great assistance to you and your kids.

Boys as well as girls need positive male and female role models. I hope you are part of a church family that has good men and women, young or old, who can fill in the gap. If not, you may need to find another church.

I had several men who stood in the gap for me. My granddad played a big role in shaping me as a man. In addition, after church, I would go home with one of the deacons sometimes. Deacon James and I had a wonderful (and sometimes a little dangerous) time. He was like a dad to me, even though I also had my biological father, who was in my life and still is. My Uncle Herndon was also my football coach in Little League. Often, he would take me and his son out and throw the football with us. All these men and others helped me develop into manhood. It may not be one person who fills the father role all the time; you may need several to assist when they can or at different seasons in your child's life.

Try to have your son with a positive male role model two hours a week. This is important to start when the child reaches between the ages of four and six, because a boy generally withdraws from Mom and identifies more with Dad during this period (if the father is available and makes the son feel loved). If a father figure cannot be there for two hours a week, then try two hours every two weeks or a month. Some time is better than no time. A mom cannot be both mom and dad.

Those families who are able to include children from single-parent (or even no-parent) homes in their family's adventures should do so sometimes, for this is pleasing to God. Uncles, grandparents, aunts, and mature youth should take time to have the kids and give the mothers a break to emotionally and physically recharge. I hear a lot of people say we just need Jesus, but I think sometimes we forget that we are Jesus's body. "Now you are the body of Christ, and each one of you is a part of it" (1 Corinthians 2:27 NIV). In other words, we are often the Jesus that someone needs to help him or her spiritually, physically, financially, and emotionally.

With today's high demand for our children to have more stuff, it is easy to put unnecessary stress on ourselves by living in an area that is too expensive. This can cause a ripple effect of buying clothes, vehicles, games, and ultimately a lifestyle that you have to constantly work extra hours to maintain. This is very bad for your children; the reality is that your children need you more than they need stuff. In addition, they need you happy and healthy in order to provide the love and loving environment they need emotionally. "Here's what you need to realize as a Mom. Your children don't want (or need) a lovely home, nice clothes, piano or gymnastics lessons. They want YOU. The best gift that you can give them is a calmer, happier, less stressed YOU" (Meeker, 2016).

"Better a small serving of vegetables with love than a fattened calf with hatred" (Proverbs 15:17 NIV).

As you are raising your children (whether they are 13 or 30), it is very important that you are doing the hard work of teaching them and training them to do for themselves whatever they are able to do. For each one shall bear his own load (Galatians 6:5 NJKV). This will help you in the long run. The saying goes, if your child is old enough to take it out, they are old enough to put it back.

If you earn enough to hire a nanny, do that by all means. However, do not forsake training your children to do what they can do. The work ethic and significance they receive from contributing to the family is invaluable.

You should not be burdened with responsibilities that your children can do for themselves. Ask the questions: Can they take clothes out of the dryer? Can they take clothes out of the washer and put them in the dryer? Can they fold and put clothes away, vacuum, sweep, mop, take out all the trash, load or unload the dishwasher, and so on? It does take time, patience, and energy to train them, but the payoff is worth it.

Requiring your children to do chores that they are capable of doing develops them to be more responsible and hardworking and will not only be an asset to you, but their future roommates and spouses will be very appreciative. Also they will be an asset to help with their younger siblings. They should not be made to be a constant babysitter, but they should be an asset.

Having daily family time for devotion is critical. Since we will reap what we sow (Galatians 6:7), it is that much more important to sow godly seeds on a daily basis so that your children not only enjoy pleasing you when you are around but enjoy pleasing God when you are not around.

If you do this correctly and start early enough, your children will not need to be constantly chaperoned as teenagers. They will qualify as people who can productively look after themselves and even look after their siblings from time to time.

Don't get distracted with dating while your children are lacking the time and attention they need. My mother started dating and got married when I was seventeen years old. I never felt that she was hard pressed for a man and put a man in front of my brother and me. That always made me feel secure. I did not truly appreciate that until I saw other mothers prioritizing a boyfriend over their own children and hurting the mother-child relationship in the process.

Whether you have one or more children as a single mother, I encourage you to stop having more children until you are married or remarried. The more children you have, the harder it is. Live pure, as God intended, and turn your heart toward God and your children. Are you praying for a spouse? Then trust God to work it out and bring a man who will be a blessing to you and your children. The right man will help your relationships with God and your children. He will also love your children as his own. The wrong man will be a stumbling block and waste your precious time. Remember, you only get a short time to invest in and raise each child. You can't afford to waste it.

If you have a problem with discipline but the children have a father or male role model who will help, you could incorporate the three-strikes-you're-out rule. This works even if you are married. When our children were disobedient or broke the rules, my wife would give our son or daughter a strike. Once they had three strikes, then I would spank them if needed. The father outside the home or the male role model can do the same. Again, I highly recommend *The New Dare to Discipline* by Dr. James Dobson to give you more insight into and details about child discipline.

As a single parent, you must realize that your children are more susceptible to sexual abuse and molestation. While you may be working and trying to find someone to watch them at the lowest rate possible, be mindful that the value of being protected from sexual abuse is priceless.

Statistics show that one in four children experience some form of child abuse or neglect in their lifetime (Centers for Disease Control and Prevention, 2014). Sexual perpetrators report that they look for passive, quiet, troubled, lonely children from single-parent or broken homes ("Child Sexual Abuse Facts," 2016).

When your children are old enough to understand, teach them about good touch and bad touch. Ask them if anyone has touched their private parts. If they have been abused, take swift action to defend the victim and stop the perpetrator. Our children should know that their private parts are never to be fondled and they are never to touch anyone else's. We can teach them about marriage privileges later.

Children who live with a single parent who has a live-in partner are at the highest risk; they are twenty times more likely to be victims of child sexual abuse than children living with both biological parents ("Child Sexual Abuse Statistics," 2015). Do things God's way, and don't let someone move in with you who has not given his life to God and to you in marriage. If he gives no ring, he gets nothing! God and your kids are worth the sacrifice to do things right.

When choosing where to live, it may help to move close to your work, but don't just follow a job for a little more money. Try to live close to family who can help. Work a job that is close to where you choose to live, because the time you will have to spend on a long commute is too precious to spend in a car or traveling.

For extra income, consider babysitting while you're with your child. It is great if you can get paid to watch someone else's child while you take care of your own and possibly give your child a playmate. At the same time, keep in mind that children can be sexually abused by other children, especially when the perpetrator is older than the victim. So be careful and be wise. "Behold, I send you out as sheep in the midst of wolves. Therefore be wise as serpents and harmless as doves" (Matthew 10:16 NKJV).

Put your children to bed at a good time in order to give yourself time to relax. Even taking thirty minutes a day can help give your mind the serenity it needs to function. Use the time to stop doing chores and really relax.

As Christians, we should be the first ones to help out the single moms in our family. Our brothers, sisters, nieces, and nephews need us. If we can help even a little with our extended cousins and family, it is pleasing to God to do so as long as we do not neglect our own.

"If any believing man or woman has widows, let them relieve them, and do not let the church be burdened, that it may relieve those who are really widows" (1 Timothy 5:16 NKJV).

I've seen sad cases where the father and the mother abandon their children. I want to encourage you if you are a single parent; you can do the job of parenting with God's help. We all need help whether we are single, married, separated, or complicated. Your sacrifice for your children is worth it. You can do it! Profess out loud. "I can do all things through Christ who strengthens me" (Philippians 4:13 NKJV).

Chapter 19

A Word from God for Grandparents

I am reminded of your sincere faith, which first lived
in your grandmother Lois and in your mother Eunice
and, I am persuaded, now lives in you also.
—2 Timothy 1:5 (NIV)

With often two parents working, so many children being born out of wedlock, and about half of the marriages ending in divorce, we are living in a time where children are relying on help from grandparents now more than ever. Sometimes grandparents are more involved in the children's lives than their own parents. Since this is the case, one grandparent or both grandparents could be the one to "train up a [grand] child in the way he should go so that when he is old he won't depart from it" (Proverbs 22:6 NKJV).

I heard Pastor John Hagee say, "Your grandchildren are your reward for not killing your own children." Chances are, as a grandparent, you are wiser than you were as a parent. Therefore, it is almost as if you are given a chance to make right the things you did wrong. I'm not saying you should necessarily take on the responsibility of the parents (which you might need to do); I'm saying you have an opportunity to give your grandchildren the care that you may not have known to give as a parent. You may have made a lot of mistakes as a parent, but now you are needed as a grandparent and you can help financially, physically, spiritually, and relationally. It is pleasing to God to help your children and grandchildren. "But if a widow has children or grandchildren, these should learn first of all to put their religion into practice by caring for their own family and so repaying their parents and grandparents, for this is pleasing to God" (1 Timothy 5:4 NIV).

You may have fallen into the false belief that there are no manuals for raising children. Maybe you did not have access to any manuals or good examples growing up, or maybe no one explained to you the scriptures that apply to parenting. Knowing what you know now, I bet you would do things differently.

"Make the most of every opportunity, because the days are evil" (Ephesians 5:16 NIV).

Consider each grandchild an opportunity to help make a new disciple for Christ. Grandparents are often feeding the kids when they come over, but are they feeding them the Word? You should make it a priority that when your grandchildren come into your presence, they will have seeds of the Word of God sown into them. As mentioned in an earlier chapter, each child needs daily bread. This means children should have at least two to five minutes a day going over one or more Bible scriptures.

Would Nana or Papa ever let a grandchild starve of physical food? Of course not! Then we cannot let them be starved of spiritual food. Job said, "Neither have I gone back from the commandment of his (God's) lips; I have esteemed the words of his mouth more than my necessary food" (Job 23:12 KJV). Job received a second chance to raise children in his older years. His first set of children, ten in all, were killed by a tornado that collapsed the roof on them while they were partying and drinking (Job 1:18–19).

Job did not have children that he could say were faithful to God. After they had birthday parties with eating and drinking, which he was not attending, he sacrificed a burnt offering for them because he thought they might have sinned and cursed God in their hearts (Job 1:4–5). Maybe Job's children were not known to be faithful to God because Job's wife did not stay faithful to God. In the time of temptation, her advice to her husband Job was "Curse God and die" (Job 2:9 NKJV). Talk about not having the godly support of your spouse. More about Job later.

With so many single-mother households, Granddad may be the only regular male voice (if he is around). If you are a grandfather, please know that you are a much more powerful influence than you might realize. Whether you are on the couch or cutting the grass, you are being watched. Grandsons are wondering what it is to be a man, and granddaughters are wondering what type of man is a good man. They need you to be there and be active. If your grandchild's father is not as involved as he should be, or he is not a good role model, it is that much more critical for you to be there at your grandchild's game, recital, or event. He or she needs affirmation, attention, and affection from a positive male as well as female parent. Even praying and reading the Word in the home with them is critical. Don't just leave it up to the grandmom or the mom. Pastor Jentezen Franklin quoted the statistic in 2016 that if just a mother goes to church, the children are 25 percent likely to continue going, but if the father goes, the children are 75 percent likely to continue going. Your presence and involvement can have an eternal impact on the soul of your grandkids.

Maybe your children are grown adults but they are not living for God. Maybe you got saved later in life. Maybe you do not have a daily devotion at home or never knew you were supposed to. Well, now you have a brand-new opportunity to sow the right seeds in your grandchildren and give them daily bread.

When you take on Job's attitude with your second set of children (grandchildren), then you may have the success he had with his second set of children. Job had another ten kids in his second set, and the girls were the most beautiful in the land (just like your grandkids ☺). The three girls received an inheritance no different than their brothers'. Job was even blessed to see his great-grandchildren (Job 42:12–17 NIV).

Even if your children are out of the home, have a daily time of devotion. If the grandkids are in your house, make sure they are included in that devotion time. Use a children's Bible or age-appropriate Bible for them. If they are old enough, they can pull up Biblegateway.com on their phone or another Bible app. If they are only there for a brief time, ask them to quote a memory verse or teach them one. Ask them about how their devotions at home are going and ask about their relationship with God.

Unfortunately most Christian grandparents only ask their grandchildren how they are doing in school, sports, or another extracurricular activity. This has only further emphasized the view that the relationship with God is of less importance than other things. Even pastoral grandparents have done this, unaware of the message they are sending to their grandchildren.

Often, grandparents allow troubled members of their family to live with them. If you do this, don't simply allow someone to stay with you; allow your home to be a place of rehabilitation. Require everyone in your house to be included in your daily devotional and prayer. Let God work on them as He works on you. We are all a work in progress, but the difference is some of us are growing closer to God and getting better while others are just getting older. Do all that is within your power to make sure that everyone who lives in your home is getting better even if it is just a little better each day.

"I planted the seed, Apollos watered it, but God has been making it grow" (1 Corinthians 3:6 NIV). God's job is to make the seed grow, but it is our job to plant and water it. If you allow someone to stay in your home, you set the guidelines. The least they can do is be there to listen to the prayer you pray and hear the Word of God you speak for two to five minutes every day or evening. It can definitely last longer, but I suggest no longer than thirty minutes of teaching. Long lectures can be tuned out after a while. As long as you are planting godly seeds daily by showing love and feeding daily bread, you're doing your part.

Children are now highly engaged in movies, music, video games, the Internet, phones, and social media. Do what you can to make sure what they are into is age appropriate. When the grandkids are with you and they say, "Grandma, can I watch this?" one of the first things you should do is ask, "What is it rated?" The same eight principles apply for the grandparents as they did for parents and guardians. And rule 8 is "Never let your children stay under ungodly influence." Give them games, movies, music, and so on that is appropriate for their age. Find something that is fun yet helps them grow. Even if it does not necessarily help them grow, it should not be something that perverts their minds or gives them the wrong messages under your watch.

The number-one responsibility of grandparents is to do everything reasonable within their power to make sure their grandchildren develop a relationship with God through the Lord Jesus Christ. Is that what you have shown is most important to your grandchildren? Will you need to change some things so they receive that message loud and clear?

If you apply these things, you will be playing a major role in changing your family and this nation for the better. You will build a legacy that can last from now until eternity.

"These are the commands, decrees and laws the LORD your God directed me to teach you … so that you, your children and their children after them may fear the LORD your God as long as you live by keeping all his decrees and commands that I give you, and so that you may enjoy long life" (Deuteronomy 6:1–2 NIV).

Let me tell you a true story of how through faith in God, my Granddad brought about a miracle for me. At the age of six, I was run over by a car. It was Sunday afternoon in June of 1986. I saw the car and tried to stop but with my dress shoes on I slipped onto my back. The car never saw me. We were in a neighborhood and thinking I was a speed bump the weight of the front tire rolled over my waist, followed by the weight of the back tire. I was completely paralyzed from the waist down.

They called the ambulance and the doctors took x-rays and did all that they could do. My mother, who was a supervisor at Doctor's West Hospital, took me to several doctors but the best solution they could come up with was a wheelchair. With their best efforts my legs were still completely paralyzed. They said they did not know if I would ever walk again, but I should feel lucky to be alive.

My Granddad, Bishop John W. Lee believed in the healing resurrection power of Jesus Christ. He and the saints at the church prayed for my healing. After a week in the hospital, they released me still paralyzed in a wheelchair. From what I remember, my mother mainly moved me around for about another week after I left the hospital. When I was home the next weekend, I was sitting down and Granddad was sitting across from me. He addressed me directly saying, "Jamar, do you believe Jesus can heal you?" "Yes." I responded. "Well then get up in Jesus name." he said. At that moment as I tried to get up, I felt strength in my legs for the first time since I was run over. It was a miracle!

I could barely stand holding on to something, but a miracle had taken place still the same. I actually had to learn how to walk all over again. Yet, every single day I got better and better. In about 3 months I was completely healed! I could run, jump, and everything else. I did not need a wheelchair, crutches, or cane, and I did not even have a limp! Glory to God the Father and His Son Jesus Christ!

I went on to win the MVP trophy on defense in little league football. At the age of 15 I won first place in the 15-18 Columbus City Diving competition. Yes I'm a Black American, and I dive (and swim for that matter). I enjoyed a wonderful childhood and even adult life full of sports awards. I was able to have 3 beautiful children with my wife and I can even dunk a basketball. Without Granddad's teaching and faith in Jesus I may still be in a wheelchair today. Thank God for grandparents! Rest in peace Granddad.

Chapter 20

You Will Reap What You Sow

Do not be deceived, God is not mocked; for whatever a
man sows, that he will also reap. For he who sows to his
flesh will of the flesh reap corruption, but he who sows
to the Spirit will of the Spirit reap everlasting life.
—Galatians 6:7–8 NKJV

This is a law and a promise that is guaranteed. You cannot sow apple seeds and get oranges, and you cannot sow orange seeds and receive apples. You will reap what you sow! You may ask, "Well, if we have brought our children to church and the preacher and teachers have sown spiritual things in them, why don't we always reap children who pursue spiritual things? Good question. That is what this chapter is all about.

First let us analyze how to reap what we sow with natural plants. I grew tomatoes with my children, and one of the first things you need to know to reap a tomato is that they grow in the summer season. Where I live in Columbus, Ohio, if you want to guarantee your tomatoes grow, you have a window of opportunity to plant the seeds. In the same way, if you want to guarantee your children go to heaven, you have a window of opportunity to plant the right seeds.

In order to guarantee your child remains committed to the Lord Jesus Christ and does not live in sin, you need to start planting the correct seeds by three years of age. However, even if you start after three years of age, your child still may stay with Christ and might never live in sin, but it is not necessarily guaranteed. This is because you reap what you sow.

If you have not been sowing the seeds to spend time with God and His Word on a daily basis, then you have been training them to put something else first on a daily basis. Those seeds will most likely bear fruit. If you have been just going to church every Sunday, then you have been training a religion and not a close relationship for the first three years of the child's life. Starting before the child turns four years of age is important. For the best results, training should start in the womb. The earlier the better.

Samuel began his training about three years of age.

In 1 Samuel 1:22b (NKJV), it says, "Not until the child is weaned; then I will take him, that he may appear before the Lord, and remain there forever."

According to Ray Fowler, "the normal time for weaning in those days was about three years (yes, just a little longer than today!), so Samuel would only have been about three years old when Hannah brought him to the temple" (Fowler, 2016).

"Then Elkanah went to his house at Ramah, but the child ministered to the Lord before Eli the priest" (1 Samuel 2:11 NKJV). The word "ministered" in this verse is the Hebrew word *Sharath*, which means "served." This is saying Samuel was actively serving as a boy. He did what the priest did as a boy. As parents, we need our child to serve the Lord as a three-year-old. At home, our children should be praying, singing worship songs, and reading the Bible with us (remember, a children's Bible or Bible app with pictures), as well as blessing their food.

If you are doing these things, then you are training your child in the way he or she should go. If you are training your child only to spend time with God when your child blesses his or her food, when your child gets older, he or she will not depart from only blessing his or her food. The problem is we have many who live a life of sin yet continue to bless their food because that was the only daily spiritual training they received. If you train your children to pray, read their Bible, worship the Lord (which includes helping the needy), and bless their food from the age of three, they will not stop doing just that when they get old. What you sow you will reap.

Most of us want our children to serve the Lord when they get older, but we do not train our children to serve the Lord daily when they are younger (again, just taking them to church twice a week is not training). Then when they turn thirteen or so and we want them to commit to fully serving the Lord on their own, they too often decide, "I'll do it when I get older." That was the seed that was sown in them, and this is the fruit of it. This is the mind-set of many individuals who have some Christian background. Unfortunately, many do not decide to fully commit to Jesus even when they get older. If we are not getting the fruit we want, we must check the seed we sowed.

Theological Questions

At this time, I would like to answer some frequently asked theological questions.

What if I did not start when my child was three or even thirteen? Do I still have hope?

Absolutely. Just start now. It's better late than never. Believe God; you will reap the spiritual seeds you sow in your child daily. Even if you didn't train your children in the way they should go, they can still get saved because you have sown the Word of God into them. This is why many who leave the church return to God. And it's never too late to pray for your loved ones to be saved. My father was saved in his fifties. Some are saved in their eighties and up.

Galatians 7:8b (NKJV) says, "He who sows to the Spirit will of the Spirit reap everlasting life."

Do all children go to heaven if they unfortunately die as children?

Yes. All children go to heaven while they are still children, before they reach the age of accountability.

"Blessed are the pure in heart, For they shall see God" (Matthew 5:8 NKJV).

Jesus said, "Let the little children come to me, and do not hinder them, for the kingdom of heaven belongs to such as these" (Matthew 19:14 NIV).

What is the age of accountability?

First, it's important to know that God is the only one who completely knows the age He will hold us accountable and how we will all be judged.

"For God will bring every deed into judgment, including every hidden thing, whether it is good or evil" (Ecclesiastes 12:14 NIV).

Based on my research as a theologian, I believe the age of accountability varies between individuals because our minds develop at different paces. We reach puberty at different times, generally between the ages of nine and fourteen. In the book *Judaism*, Sue Penny describes how in Jewish culture, a boy becomes a bar mitzvah (son of the commandments) at the age of thirteen. Once he has reached the age of bar mitzvah, a Jewish boy is counted as a man and is no longer a child. A girl becomes a bat mitzvah (daughter of the commandments) automatically at the age of twelve and is now a woman (Penny, 1997). It is common for girls to go through puberty and mature mentally and physically before boys.

I believe we become accountable and are endanger of going to hell after puberty and when we truly know right from wrong. This is probably around twelve or thirteen years of age (only God knows for sure). At the age of about twelve, Jesus said he must be about his Father's business (see Luke 2:42–52 for the whole story).

"Therefore, to him who knows to do good and does not do it, to him it is sin" (James 4:17 NKJV).

Can a child be baptized? How early?

Once children have knowledge enough to understand the gospel, they are a candidate for baptism. If they believe Jesus is the Son of God, died for their sin, and rose again, and they repent from whatever wrong they have done and truly confess Jesus as their Lord, they should be baptized out of obedience to the Lord Jesus Christ. It needs to be the child's decision and not the parent's decision. The child should have enough knowledge to make a conscious decision. The word *conscious* means "with knowledge."

"There is also an antitype which now saves us—baptism (not the removal of the filth of the flesh, but the answer of a good conscience toward God), through the resurrection of Jesus Christ" (1 Peter 3:21 NKJV).

This also means that a baby is not a candidate for true baptism. If a baby has a ceremony (or baptism), he or she still needs to decide to repent and be baptized on his or her own accord when he or she is old enough to do so. Someone who can understand sin and can repent can then be baptized.

"Peter replied, 'Repent and be baptized, every one of you, in the name of Jesus Christ for the forgiveness of your sins. And you will receive the gift of the Holy Spirit. The promise is for you and your children and for all who are far off—for all whom the Lord our God will call" (Acts 2:38–39 NIV).

It is my stance that I will not baptize anyone under five years old so the child has a better understanding. I made my children wait even longer so they had a deeper comprehension and so others would have more respect for their decision when they shared their faith in the future. Our son Judah was baptized in water when he turned eight years of age, and my daughter, Jael, was baptized at nine years of age. Even though our son received the baptism of the Holy Spirit when he was five years old and wanted to be baptized in water then, I made him wait to be baptized in water for the reasons I mentioned above. With God's guidance, my wife, Cassandra, and I developed all three of our children to have a hunger and thirst after righteousness as early as I can remember. If you follow the directions in this book with the leading of the Holy Spirit, God guarantees your children will pursue God at an early age and into eternity as well.

When will I know if my children have truly given their life to Christ?

Allow me share an excerpt from Luis and Pat Palau in the book *Keeping Your Kids Christian* (1990).

> Children raised in Christian homes often commit their lives to the Lord Jesus several times in different ways as they're growing up. If you ask them when they became a Christian, they'll probably say, "The earliest decision I can remember is …" Others, like Billy Graham's wife Ruth, say they can't remember a specific day when they received Christ, but they can't remember a day when they didn't trust him either.

Consider this analogy. When did my son truly accept me as his earthly father? My son told me he can't remember a time he did not accept me as his father. If you are a father or mother and you love your children properly, they will accept you as their father or mother. Children really do not get to choose who their parents are, and if we are their parents, we should not let them choose. We should let them know the truth, that we are their father and mother as soon as possible.

In the same way, God is our Father and their Father in heaven, and we should let our children know this as soon as possible. We should teach them the truth—that Jesus is the Son of God and He is the Lord and Savior of the world. "God also has highly exalted Him and given Him the name which is above every name, that at the name of Jesus every knee should bow, of those in heaven, and of those on earth, and of those under the earth, and that every tongue should confess that Jesus Christ is Lord, to the glory of God the Father" (Philippians 2:9–11 NKJV).

"By their fruits you will know them" (Matthew 7:20).

You can look for fruits, but don't wait for fruits. Treat them as true converts. Our job is not to produce the fruits in them; our job is to plant the seeds, water them, and let God increase the fruit. Paul said, "I planted, Apollos watered, but God gave the increase" (1 Corinthians 3:6). Do not wait to see if your child will spend more time in prayer or more time reading God's Word or show more love to his or her sibling or be more obedient. Train these habits into your child.

After my son was baptized, I gave him a model prayer for him to say each morning as Jesus did with His disciples. My daughter, who was six at the time, asked for a model prayer as well. I was overjoyed to provide one for her.

Should I let my children choose their own faith?

I know some parents who say they want to let their children choose their own faith. That would be like me saying I will let my child refer to me as "Jamar" and if he wants to call me "Dad" when he's old enough, then I will let him choose to call me Dad. If I start training my son from birth to call me Jamar, he will call me Jamar. In essence, I would be training him not to accept me as dad.

Remember, we are training our children no matter what we do. Therefore, if I have to choose whether to train my son *not* to accept me as his father or to accept me as his father, why would I start off training him not to accept me as his father? Similarly, why would we train our children not to accept God as their heavenly Father and Jesus as their Lord starting off? Yet that is exactly what we are doing when we say we will let them choose their Lord when they are older. When parents do this, they sow seeds of rejecting Christ in the beginning, and that is often what they reap in the end.

So when should you teach them that Jesus is Lord? The same time you teach your children that you are their parent. As early as possible, starting in the womb. It is the truth, and our children need to know this truth from the start. Jesus said, "And you shall know the truth, and the truth shall make you free" (John 8:32 NKJV), and "I am the way, the truth, and the life. No one comes to the Father except through Me" (John 14:6 NKJV).

Can I really force my child to choose Jesus as their Lord?

No, and you do not need to force children to choose Jesus or force them to desire the things of God. People are born with a desire to worship God (as well as a sinful nature); that is why many create their own god. If they do not choose a god, they make themselves their own god and create their own right and wrong. You are introducing your children and training them on how to serve Yahweh, the one true God, the Creator of heaven and earth, through a relationship with His Son, the Lord Jesus Christ. In 1 Peter 2:2–3 (NIV), it says, "Like newborn babies, crave pure spiritual milk, so that by it you may grow up in your salvation, now that you have tasted that the Lord is good."

Like babies desire natural milk, they also desire spiritual milk. We are a spirit, we have a soul, and we live in a body. Both our spirits and bodies need milk. If a baby is not fed physically, that baby will cry for food. I believe that if the baby is not fed spiritually, the baby will cry for spiritual food also. This is one reason why babies may cry even after all their physical needs are met. You may have changed their diaper, fed them, gave them comfortable clothes, made sure they're not too hot or cold, rocked them, and done everything naturally necessary, yet the baby is still crying.

If your pediatrician finds no medical reason for the crying, then he or she will say your baby has colic. According to the University of Michigan Health System, some experts estimate about half of all babies have colic (Boyse, 2010).

This basically means that the baby will just cry for no explainable reason and there is nothing you can really do about it until he or she grows out of it. I'm saying that your baby needs to receive the spiritual milk of the Word daily and sometimes they will cry because that is what they are craving. I am not a medical doctor, but I am an ordained minister of God. Sometimes your son or daughter may need medicine for physical, emotional, or mental issues. I recommend you consult your doctor and that you read the Word of God to your son or daughter daily. My own children have literally stopped crying before when I have prayed and spoken God's Word over them. Of course, we must assess all their needs, both natural and spiritual, and not neglect either. Most parents attend the natural but miss the spiritual.

Do our children really have a choice?

"You did not choose me, but I chose you and appointed you to go and bear fruit—fruit that will last. Then the Father will give you whatever you ask in my name" (John 15:16 NIV). The choice is not completely up to the child, no more than who their parents are is. If the parents choose them, they are chosen and they will choose Christ. At the same time, ultimately they will choose how much fruit they bear.

"But these are the ones sown on good ground, those who hear the word, accept it, and bear fruit: some thirtyfold, some sixty, and some a hundred" (Mark 4:20 NKJV).

We do have many choices in life, but there are a lot of things that we cannot choose. We cannot choose our biological parents. We cannot choose where we are born. We did not choose to be birthed on this earth. We cannot choose whether God created us or whether Jesus is the Lord of all. These are things established whether we choose to believe them or not.

Did the nation of Israel choose to be blessed, or are they blessed because of their father Abraham? Look at what God told Isaac: "I will make your descendants multiply as the stars of heaven; I will give to your descendants all these lands; and in your seed all the nations of the earth shall be blessed; because Abraham obeyed My voice and kept My charge, My commandments, My statutes, and My laws" (Genesis 26:4–5 NKJV). God chose Abraham because of how he would raise his children. "For I have chosen him, so that he will direct his children and his household after him to keep the way of the LORD by doing what is right and just, so that the LORD will bring about for Abraham what he has promised him" (Genesis 18:19 NIV).

Did Samuel have a choice to be dedicated to God's service, or did his mother determine that? His mother says, "'I prayed for this child, and the LORD has granted me what I asked of him. So now I give him to the LORD. For his whole life he will be given over to the LORD.' And he worshiped the LORD there" (1 Samuel 1:27–28 NKJV).

Did John the Baptist have a choice whether he was born with the Holy Spirit?

"You shall call his name John. And you will have joy and gladness, and many will rejoice at his birth. For he will be great in the sight of the Lord, and shall drink neither wine nor strong drink. He will also be filled with the Holy Spirit, even from his mother's womb" (Luke 1:13–15 NKJV).

Our children will have about as much choice to live for God as John the Baptist and Samuel did, yet they will have more of a choice on how much fruit they bear for Christ.

We will reap what we sow and what other influences sow. If we don't like the fruit, we must go past the root and examine the seeds.

Chapter 21

WWJPD—What Would Jesus's Parents Do?

> Then the angel said to her, "Do not be afraid, Mary, for you
> have found favor with God. And behold, you will conceive in
> your womb and bring forth a Son, and shall call His name Jesus.
> He will be great, and will be called the Son of the Highest;
> Luke 1:30-32a (NKJV)

C an you believe that God chose natural, imperfect parents to raise his only begotten Son? Many people are asking the question "What Would Jesus Do (WWJD)?" As parents, if we want children who will follow in Jesus's footsteps, we should be asking the question "What Would Jesus's Parents Do (WWJPD)?" What better mother and father to pattern after than the parents God picked? In this chapter, we will see how they followed the eight principles to make sure Jesus was successful in education and salvation and overcame temptation.

Principle 1—Commit Each Child to God

"Now when the days of her purification according to the law of Moses were completed, they brought Him to Jerusalem to present Him to the Lord (as it is written in the law of the Lord, 'Every male who opens the womb shall be called holy to the Lord')" (Luke 2:22–23 NKJV).

They committed Jesus to God. Every Jew was required to commit his or her firstborn son to God, and he was called "holy to the Lord." Now we are to commit all our children to the Lord, and they all are to be called holy, male and female, the first to the last. All our children are to be consecrated and set apart for God.

"For the unbelieving husband is sanctified by the wife, and the unbelieving wife is sanctified by the husband; otherwise your children would be unclean, but now they are holy" (1 Corinthians 7:14 NKJV).

Principle 2—Holiness Lived in Front of Them

"When Joseph and Mary had done everything required by the Law of the Lord, they returned to Galilee to their own town of Nazareth" (Luke 2:39 NIV).

Joseph and Mary did everything required by the law. They lived according to God's law, and Jesus saw an example of holiness lived in front of Him.

Principle 3—Instruct and Train Your Children in the Way They Should Go

"And the child grew and became strong; he was filled with wisdom, and the grace of God was on him" (Luke 2:40 NIV).

Luke 2:39 said they did everything required by the law, which means they kept the most important commandment, Deuteronomy 6:5–9 (NIV):

> Love the Lord your God with all your heart and with all your soul and with all your strength. These commandments that I give you today are to be upon your hearts. Impress them on your children. Talk about them when you sit at home and when you walk along the road, when you lie down and when you get up. Tie

them as symbols on your hands and bind them on your foreheads. Write them on the doorframes of your houses and on your gates.

Principle 4—Love and Esteem Your Spouse Properly

"And Joseph her husband, being a righteous man and not wanting to disgrace her, planned to send her away secretly" (Matthew 1:19 NASB).

Men who truly love their women God's way will not try to sleep with them before they are married and disgrace them. Joseph demonstrated loving his spouse properly by being unselfish. Instead of making it known to everyone their separation was not his fault but was Mary's fault for cheating, he kept the reason a secret. Even after she became pregnant with someone else's baby and he felt completely betrayed, Joseph protected his wife and sought to put her away privately. He was so concerned about Mary he was not disclosing the specific reason for separation. Therefore, she could not be stoned or shunned on his account. He is an example of how a man should love a woman.

Principle 5—Declare Your Child's Future

"And she will bring forth a Son, and you shall call His name Jesus, for He will save His people from their sins" (Matthew 1:21 NKJV).

God declared Jesus's future, saying, "He will save His people from their sins." He also reiterated how important the name is; therefore, He named Jesus Himself.

Jesus is the Greek form of Joshua (Yoshua in Hebrew), which means, "The Lord saves" (NASB, 1999).

Principle 6—Receive Resources on Marriage and Family Regularly

"Plans fail for lack of counsel, but with many advisers they succeed" (Proverbs 15:22 NIV).

They read the books of Moses and the Proverbs, which gave them directions and instructions on marriage and family, such as the following:

- Deuteronomy 24:5 (NKJV): "When a man has taken a new wife, he shall not go out to war or be charged with any business; he shall be free at home one year, and bring happiness to his wife whom he has taken."
- Deuteronomy 6:6–7 (NKJV): "These commandments that I give you today are to be on your hearts. Impress them on your children. Talk about them when you sit at home and when you walk along the road, when you lie down and when you get up."
- Proverbs 22:6 (NKJV): "Train up a child in the way he should go, And when he is old he will not depart from it."

Principle 7—Esteem and Love Your Child Properly

"An angel of the Lord appeared to Joseph in a dream, saying, 'Arise, take the young Child and His mother, flee to Egypt, and stay there until I bring you word; for Herod will seek the young Child to destroy Him.'

When he arose, he took the young Child and His mother by night and departed for Egypt, and was there until the death of Herod, that it might be fulfilled which was spoken by the Lord through the prophet, saying, 'Out of Egypt I called My Son.'" (Matthew 2:13–15 NKJV).

This is an excellent example of Joseph and Mary esteeming and loving their children properly. They put God and their family first by obeying the direction of God, packing up quickly, and moving. They moved their whole family and livelihood in order for their child to live in a better environment.

Joseph was a carpenter with his own business. He could have said he could not leave because he had worked so hard to develop clients in that area and he would have to start from scratch. In Genesis 19, Lot was told to move with his family, but he hesitated and had to be grabbed and pulled from his home. Then Lot came up with his own place he'd rather move to instead of where God said. Lot's actions proved God's directions for his family were not his top priority.

I know too many parents who will not move even though their children are in a bad environment. There are also parents who move for a better job and unfortunately snatch their children out of a wonderful environment. Whether we stay or move, we should not decide simply based off of where we think we can make more money. We must put God and our families' best interests first.

As mentioned in previous chapters, putting God first does not mean putting the church or the ministry first. Dr. James Dobson was called "the nation's most influential evangelical leader" by the *New York Times* (Kirkpatrick, 2005), but have you heard of his father? His father was a traveling minister who was not able to be home often. Dr. Dobson's mom was having trouble with raising young Jim without his father around. When she let his father, James C Dobson Sr. know that she and Jim needed him home, Evangelist Dobson Sr. stopped his traveling ministry and took a pastoral job in order to be home more.

Since Dobson Sr. sacrificed his fame and finances and focused on his family more than his ministry, our nation has reaped the benefits through his son. Dr. James Dobson Jr. He founded Focus on the Family and continues to transform countless families for the better through various books and ministries. What a legacy Pastor Dobson Sr. left. Most important, Pastor Dobson's children and his grandchildren live for God. Do not put your ministry, business, job, or career before your immediate family.

Imagine having your toddler in a neighborhood full of violence, a place where murder takes place on a regular basis and where the government is so corrupt that the police are the ones murdering kids at will. Talk about a bad neighborhood. As a toddler, this is the very environment Jesus was in. Even though God has all power and is able to do miraculous things, He left it up to Jesus's natural mom and stepdad to follow His directions to keep Baby Jesus safe.

I must admit, I would have been inclined to suggest that God send down some more guardian angels to post around the house. I might have asked God to send a plague or two to warn King Herod not to mess with us. Yet, Joseph trusted that God's plans were the best plans to fulfill God's ultimate purpose in his life as well as his family's.

Many times, we are praying for a miracle when most of the time God answers with a principle. If your children are constantly threatened verbally or physically by their environment, you should probably move. It may be rough to do, but your children are worth it, especially in an atmosphere that could seriously threaten their salvation.

Jesus was not born full of wisdom. I know it is hard to imagine, but our Lord and Savior could not even speak when He came into this world. He was actually taught how to walk, talk, read, and write. So how did He get so much wisdom? Was it simply because He was God's Son? That did have something to do with it, but the Bible says that He did not start off full of wisdom but that through teaching, his parents filled Him with Wisdom. His parents poured wisdom into him through the Word and prayer. Luke 2:40 says, "And the child grew and became strong; he was filled with wisdom, and the grace of God was upon him."

Instead of dealing with a rebellious child at twelve years old, you can have an obedient child desiring to do God's will. Look at Joseph and Mary's twelve-year results. Luke 2:46–48, 51–52 (NIV) says,

> After three days they found him in the temple courts, sitting among the teachers, listening to them and asking them questions. Everyone who heard him was amazed at his understanding and his answers. When his parents

saw him, they were astonished … Then he went down to Nazareth with them and was obedient to them. But his mother treasured all these things in her heart. And Jesus grew in wisdom and stature, and in favor with God and men.

Principle 8—Never Let Your Child Stay under Ungodly Influence

"When he arose, he took the young Child and His mother by night and departed for Egypt, and was there until the death of Herod" (Matthew 2:14 NKJV).

Again, when Jesus was in a negative environment, they moved him without hesitation. As you hear from God while going through this book, do not hesitate to make the changes He directs you to make.

"And the Child grew and became strong in spirit, filled with wisdom; and the grace of God was upon Him" (Luke 2:40 NKJV).

Remember Jesus's parents did everything required by the law; therefore, we know that they impressed the commandments at home. Being a Jewish boy, He was taught the Old Testament in school, as was the custom. When He was about the age of twelve or thirteen, His parents really got to see the budding of the seeds that had been sown in their child. A true test of what is in our child's heart is what he or she does when out of our presence.

At twelve (or thirteen), when Jesus was away from his parents for three days, what was He doing?

"Now so it was that after three days they found Him in the temple, sitting in the midst of the teachers, both listening to them and asking them questions" (Luke 2:46 NKJV). He was pursuing God's will.

Although we cannot expect our children to be perfect, we can expect them to live for God as long as they live. Many others in the Bible are our examples. You will find the threads of these principles woven into the lives of Joseph, Samuel, Zadok, Jeremiah, Josiah, Mary, Timothy, Daniel, and others.

You may think they did not have as many negative influences in the previous generations. The truth is many children are trained in the way they should go in our society today and never rebel against God: Pastor John Hagee's children, Pastor Gary Keesee's kids, Dr. James Dobson's children, Ray Comfort's kids, Dr. Gary Chapman's children, Tim Tebow and his siblings, Dr. Tony Evans's children, and even my brother-in-law, who was raised by a single mom. There are many, many more. This should not be an anomaly but a normal result of Christian parenting.

We know too much now to allow our children to fall prey to the enemy of this world. The youth of our generation are not the problem; the youth in our generation are the solution to the problems. Let's pray for our parents and for the youth being raised up as an army for the kingdom of God.

Be encouraged for God says to us,

> And it shall come to pass in the last days, says God, That I will pour out of My Spirit on all flesh; Your sons and your daughters shall prophesy, Your young men shall see visions, Your old men shall dream dreams. And on My menservants and on My maidservants I will pour out My Spirit in those days; And they shall prophesy. (Acts 2:17–18 NKJV).

We are warriors destined to use our children as arrows against the enemy. "Behold, children are a heritage from the LORD, The fruit of the womb is a reward. Like arrows in the hand of a warrior, So are the children of one's youth. Happy is the man who has his quiver full of them; They shall not be ashamed" (Psalm 127:3–5a NKJV).

Guarantee CHILDREN Will Go to Heaven

Commit each child to God.
Holiness lived in front of your children.
Instruct and train your children in the way they should go.
Love and esteem your spouse properly.
Declare your children's future.
Receive resources on marriage and family regularly.
Esteem and love your children properly.
Never let your children stay under ungodly influence.

In doing so, you will receive God's promise for your children from birth until burial.

"These are the commands, decrees and laws the Lord your God directed me to teach you … so that you, your children and their children after them may fear the Lord your God as long as you live by keeping all his decrees and commands that I give you, and so that you may enjoy long life" (Deuteronomy 6:1–2 NIV).

I leave you with the same prayer I pray over my children each night as I lay my hands on them. It is from Numbers 6:24–26 (NKJV)"

> The Lord bless you and keep you; The Lord make His face shine upon you, And be gracious to you; The Lord lift up His countenance upon you, And give you peace. In Jesus's name. Amen.

References

(2012). Retrieved September 2016 from Christianity.stackexchange. com. http://christianity.stackexchange.com/questions/9335/ why-is-the-word-lord-in-all-caps-in-the-ot-but-not-in-the-nt.

Advocate. (1993). "Gay Matter." *Advocate* 630.

American Psychological Association. (2010). 6th Edition. American Pyschological Association.

Beers, V. Gilbert. (1990). *Keeping Your Kids Christian*. Ann Arbor, MI: Servant Publications.

Blue Letter Bible. "Train." (2016). Retrieved 2016, from blueletterbible. org: https://www.blueletterbible.org.

Boyse, K. (2010). "Your Child Development and Behavior Resources: Colic." Retrieved September 2016. http://www.med.umich. edu/1libr/yourchild/colic.htm.

CARM. (2009). "Can We Trust the New Testament." Retrieved 2013. http:// carm.org/can-we-trust-new-testament-historical-document.

Carson, Ben. (2011). Circa" Ben Carson: I Will Believe in Evolution When They Show Me the Fossils" http://gawker.com/ben-carson-i-will-believe-in-evolution-when-they-show-1740908238.

Centers for Disease Control and Prevention. (2014). "Violence Prevention." Retrieved September 2016. http://www.cdc.gov/ViolencePrevention/childmaltreatment/index.html.

Centers for Disease Control and Prevention. (2016). "Suicide Statistics." Retrieved April 2016. http://www.cdc.gov/violenceprevention/suicide/statistics/index.html.

Chapman, D. G. (2015). *The Five Love Languages: The Secret to Love That Lasts*. Chicago: Northfield Publishing.

Chapman, G., and A. Pellicane. (2014). *Growing Up Social: Raising Relational Kids in a Screen-Driven World*. Chicago: Northfield Publishing.

Chapman, M. W. (2015). "Dr. Carson on Evolution: 'No One Has Ever Demonstrated One Species Changing to Another Species.'" CNS News. Retrieved September 2016. http://www.cnsnews.com/blog/michael-w-chapman/dr-carson-evolution-no-one-has-ever-demonstrated-one-species-changing-another.

Chen, G. (2015). "Public School Verus Private School." Retrieved September 2016. http://www.publicschoolreview.com/blog/public-school-vs-private-school.

"Child Sexual Abuse Facts." (2016). Retrieved September 2016. http://cachouston.org/child-sexual-abuse-facts/%202016.

"Child Sexual Abuse Statistics." (2015). Darkness to Light. Retrieved September 2016. http://www.d2l.org/atf/cf/%7B64AF78C4-5EB8-45AA-BC28-F7EE2B581919%7D/Statistics_4_Risk_Factors.pdf.

Comfort, R. (2013). "How to Bring Your Children to Christ … and Keep Them There." Retrieved August 2016. https://www.youtube.com/watch?v=i2PotrHVnis.

Common Sense Media. (2016). Retrieved 2016. https://www. commonsensemedia.org/about-us/our-mission#about-us.

Dallas, J. (2003). *Desires in Conflict: Hope for Men Who Struggle with Sexual Identity.* Eugene, Oregon: Harvest House Publishers.

Dallas, J., and N. Heche. (2010). *The Complete Christian Guide to Understanding Homosexuality.* Eugene, OR: Harvest House Publishers.

"Darwin Fish Lacks Tetrapod Legs." (2016). http://crev.info/2016/09/ darwin-fish-lacks-tetrapod-legs.

Dictionary.com (2016). "Gay." Retrieved September 2016. http://www. dictionary.com/browse/gay?s=t

Dictionary.com (2016). "Sexual Orientation." Retrieved September http://www.dictionary.com/browse/sexual-orientation?s=t

Dictionary.com. (2016). "Train." Retrieved April 2016. http://mfeed. reference.com/d/search.html?q=Train.

District of Abington Township v. Schempp. (2014). Retrieved September 2016. https://www.britannica.com/topic/School-District-of-Abington-Township-v-Schempp.

Dobson, J. (2001). *Bringing Up Boys.* Carol Stream, IL: Tyndale House.

Dobson, J. (2014). *Bringing Up Girls.* Tyndale House Publishers.

Dobson, J. (2014). *The New Dare to Discipline.* Carol Stream, IL: Tyndale House Publishers.

Dobson, J. (2014). *Your Legacy: The Greatest Gift.* New York: FaithWords.

Duplantis, J. (2012). *Distortion: The Vanity of Genetically Altered Christianity*. Grand Rapids, MI: Harrison House Publishers.

Dykman, J. (2008). "Fastest Growing Religion." *The Pew Forum on Religion and Public Life*.

Edwards v. Aguilard. (2014). https://www.britannica.com/topic/Edwards-v-Aguilard.

Fowler, R. (2016). *Samuel Dedicated to God*. Retrieved Septemeber 2016. http://www.rayfowler.org/sermons/1-samuel/dedicated-to-god/.

Hagee, J. (2014). *The Power of the Prophetic Blessing*. Brentwood, TN: Worthy Publishing.

Haynes, C. (2011). "The Truth about School Prayer." *Washington Post*. December 11. Retrieved September 2016. https://www.washingtonpost.com/blogs/answer-sheet/post/the-truth-about-school-prayer/2011/12/23/gIQAHHJoEP_blog.html.

Henry, W. (1993). "Born Gay?" *Time* 321.

History of School Prayer." (n.d.). http://www.onevoiceprayer.com/campuses/history-of-school-prayer/.

Jay-Z. (2001). "H To The Izzo." Retrieved September 2016. azlyrics.com.

Jeremiah, D. D. (2017). *Turning Point with Dr. David Jeremiah*. Retrieved January 2017. http://tbn.org/watch/live.

Keesee, Drenda. (2015). *The New Vintage Family*. New Albany: Free Indeed Publishers.

Kinsey, A. (1948). *Sexual Behavior in the Human Male*. Philadelphia, PA: Saunders Press.

Kirkpatrick, D. (2005). "Evangelical Leader Threatens to Use His Political Muscle against Some Democrats." *New York Times*. January 1. Retrieved September 2016. http://www.nytimes. com/2005/01/01/politics/evangelical-leader-threatens-to-use-his-political-muscle-against.html?_r=0.

Lerner, C. (2016). "When Does Discipline Begin? An Age-by-Age Guide to Setting Limits."

Luce, R. (2005). *Battle Cry for a Generation*.

Martin, F. P. (1996). *Hung by the Tongue*. Whitaker.

McLennan Distinguished Lecture Series. (2011). Retrieved September 2016. www.baylor.edu/research/index/php?id=84221.

Meeker, M. (2016). "A Single Mom's Cry for Help." http://www. drjamesdobson.org/blogs/dr-meeker-blog/dear-dr-meg/2016/ 05/31/a-single-mom%27s-cry-for-help.

Merriam-Webster. (2016). Retrieved 2016. http://www.merriam-webster. com/dictionary/teach.

NASB. (1999). *NASB Study Bible*. Zondervan.

Newsweek. (1990). "The Future of Gay America." *Newsweek*, 20–27.

Newsweek. (1992). "Is This Child Born Gay?" *Newsweek*, 46.

NHS UK. (2016). http://www.nhs.uk/chq/Pages/819.aspx?Category ID=52&SubCategoryID=142.

Nicolosi, J., and L. Nicolosi. (2003). *A Parent's Guide to Preventing Homosexuality*. New York: Intervarsity Press.

Nimmons, D. (1994). "Sex and the Brain." *Discover*, 122.

NIV. (n.d.). *New International Version.* Zondervan.

NKJV. (n.d.). *New King James Version.* Zondervan.

Pearl, M. A. (1994). *To Train Up A Child.* Pleasantville, TN: No Greater Joy Ministries Inc. www.nogreaterjoy.org.

Penny, S. (1997). *Judaism: Discovering Religions.* Austin, TX: Raintree Steck-Vaughn Publishers.

Pew Center. (2015). "US Public Becoming Less Religious." Religion and Public Life. http://www.pewforum.org/2015/11/03/u-s-public-becoming-less-religious/

Ramsey, Dave. (n.d.). daveramsey.com. Retrieved 2016. http://www.daveramsey.com/store/financial-peace-university/cFpu.html.

Ray, D. B. (2016). *Research Facts on Homeschooling.* Retrieved September 2016. http://www.nheri.org/research/research-facts-on-home schooling.html.

Robinson, M. N. (2016). "*Epperson v. State of Arkansas.*" Retrieved September 2016. https://www.britannica.com/topic/Epperson-v-State-of-Arkansas.

"School Prayer in America." (2013). Retrieved September 2016. http://www.schoolprayerinamerica.info/.

Six Children Raised by Animals. (2012). Retrieved October 2013 from theweek.com. http://theweek.com/article/index/235216/6-children-raised-by-animals.

Smith, D. M. (2016). *Ohio Christian University.* Ohio Chrisitan University.

"Spanking." (2016). Retrieved September 2016. http://safenaturaltips.com/spanking.html.

therefinersfire.org. (2016). "Phylacteries." Retrieved August 2016. http://www.therefinersfire.org/phylacteries.htm.

Thompson, J. (2008). "Beyoncé Explains Her Alter-Ego Sasha Fierce." *Mirror.* November 27. Retrieved September 2016. http://www.mirror.co.uk/3am/celebrity-news/beyonce-explains-her-alter-ego-sasha-fierce-362578.

Time. (2014). "The 100 Most Influential People." *Time.*

uscourts.gov. (2016). Retrieved 2016. http://www.uscourts.gov/educational-resources/educational-activities/facts-and-case-summary-engel-v-vitale.

Vicedo, M. (2013). *The Nature and Nurture of Love: From Imprinting to Attachment in Cold War America.* Chicago: University of Chicago.

Warren, R. (2002). *The Purpose Driven Life: What on Earth Am I Here For?* Grand Rapids, MI: Zondervan.

WebMD. (2012). "Sexual Orientation." Retrieved October 2013. http://www.webmd.com/sex-relationships/guide/sexual-orientation.

WFP. (2015). "Hunger Statistics." Retrieved September 2016. https://www.wfp.org/hunger/stats.

"What Happened When Prayer Was Taken out of Schools." (2009). September 26. Retrieved September 2016. http://www.sicknesshope.com/node/1075.

whattoexpect.com. (2015). "Pregnancy and Fetal Hearing." Retrieved September 2016. http://www.whattoexpect.com/pregnancy/fetal-hearing/.

www.esrb.org. (2016). www.esrb.org. Retrieved May 2016. www. esrb.org.

www.k12reader.com. (2016). www.k12reader.com. Retrieved 2016. www.k12reader.com.

yourdictionary.com. (n.d.). "Impress." Retrieved 2016. http://www. yourdictionary.com/impress.

About the Author

Rev. Jamar Haynes Lee has been in ministry for over 20 years. Jamar and his wife Cassandra are the founders of Family & Marriage Enrichment and have a heart to help families flourish. Together they also head the Youth Ministry at Glory To God Ministries in Canal Winchester, OH. Youth Pastor Jamar often demonstrates his love for others while preaching in the prisons, visiting the nursing home and hospitals, and helping the less fortunate. Using his gifts, Rev. Jamar has had the opportunity to speak and do standup comedy nationally and internationally, including touring with the legendary comedian Sinbad. He also wrote, produced, and starred in the song/video *The Graduation Anthem*. He graduated top of his class from the Young Preachers Institute and majored in Psychology with a focus on the family graduating Magna Cum Laude from Ohio Christian University. As a devoted husband and father of two boys and a girl he lives by his quote, "As you get better, your relationships will get better."

Made in the USA
San Bernardino, CA
12 July 2018